PARIS,

CITY OF ENCHANTMENT

BOOKS BY ERNEST RAYMOND

NOVELS:

A London Gallery comprising
We, the Accused
The Marsh
Gentle Greaves
The Witness of Canon Welcome
A Chorus Ending
The Kilburn Tale
Child of Norman's End
For Them That Trespass
Was There Love Once?
The Corporal of the Guard
A Song of the Tide
The Chalice and the Sword
To the Wood No More
The Lord of Wensley
The Old June Weather
The City and the Dream

Other Novels:
The Visit of Brother Ives
The Quiet Shore
The Nameless Places
Tell England
A Family that Was
The Jesting Army
Mary Leith
Morris in the Dance
The Old Tree Blossomed
Don John's Mountain Home
The Five Sons of le Faber
The Last to Rest
Newtimber Lane
The Miracle of Brean
Rossenal
Damascus Gate
Wanderlight
Daphne Bruno I
Daphne Bruno II

BIOGRAPHIES:

Two Gentlemen of Rome
(The Story of Keats and Shelley)
In the Steps of St. Francis
In the Steps of the Brontës

ESSAYS, ETC.:

Through Literature to Life
The Shout of the King
Back to Humanity (with Patrick Raymond)

PLAYS

The Berg
The Multabello Road

PARIS,
CITY OF ENCHANTMENT

by

ERNEST RAYMOND

Illustrated by Gordon Randall, R.I.

NEWNES : LONDON

First Published 1961

Text set in 12 point Garamond, 1 point leaded

Made and printed in Great Britain by
The Garden City Press Limited, Letchworth, Hertfordshire
for George Newnes Limited, Tower House
Southampton Street, Strand, W.C.2

To the Memory

of

I. A. B.

Who so loved Paris

Contents

Gordon Randall's drawings
at the opening to each chapter
illustrate the following:

List of Plates

LIST OF PLATES

1

An Island and Two Hills

1

An Island and Two Hills

To grasp the shape or " lie " of Paris, to understand its history, to enlarge the interest you bring to it, and to enrich the memories you take away from it, all you need to do, at first, is to think of an island and two hills.

It is easy: a small island in the Seine and a hill on either side of it; one a low one close to it on the southern bank; the other a high one rising some distance away on the northern shore. The Ile de la Cité; the extremely famous hill of St. Geneviève; and the once holy hill of Montmartre.

That is really all. Of course these two hills have shoulders which in the old days enclosed stretches of plain and swamp; and these fenland areas have had their part in historic and terrible things; but we shall come to that.

And if in our study of this great and haunted city we begin at its centre, the small river island, and work out-wards to the two hills we shall, by good fortune, follow the course of the history of Paris from its dawn in the breaking river mists to its vast swell, its proud brilliance, and its capital importance today.

Before the Romans came to Gaul there was this little wet island lying on a narrow loop of the yet nameless Seine, floating on it, as it were. The nameless river was deep and moved slowly through a quiet green valley. The island was mostly rushes and willows; the mainland, save where the southern hill came down close to the bank, was largely a marsh of reeds. Each of the marshy riverside strands was embraced by a crescent of wooded slopes, and each crescent rose to a summit, a low rounded one on the south (St. Geneviève); a high conical one in the north (Montmartre).

Obviously the oval island, lonely and set apart, with a natural moat around it, was a good place to defend; and accordingly the round, thatched huts of the Parisii, a Gallic tribe, gathered there among the rushes and the willows. Because the river was deep and its current slow the long-haired Parisii in their cloaks of skin or peltry became boatmen and fishermen and riparian traders; but they had a wooden bridge across to the north bank so that they could hunt game in the woods or prey on the water-birds in the marshlands or fight alongside others of their tribe in places beyond the hills.

Such was the little green basin, usually still and quiet except for the furtive steps of the hunters or the hoarse cries of the water-fowl; and yet it was destined to pack with history; to hold events so tumultuous and so potent that they changed more than once the direction of mankind.

Can we better understand how history for two thousand years has filled up this little basin than by hearing that the present Pont Notre Dame is exactly on the site of that first wooden bridge over which the Parisii clattered to their hunting or their fighting; that Notre Dame rises in all its glory above the very spot where they had an altar or some small temple to the god of their river; that the Palais de Justice on the opposite half of the island rises above their place of tribal assembly; that thus for two millennia this western end has heard the pronouncements of justice, and the eastern end the sounds of worship; and lastly that the white domes of Sacré Coeur de Montmartre crown the " high place " which the Parisii climbed so as to offer their sacrifices in its sacred grove?

A little more about the island: we must not when crossing its Parvis Notre Dame or approaching the Conciergerie along its Quai de l'Horloge walk this piece of haunted earth blind.

The Romans, marching about Gaul in the course of

Caesar's conquest, came to this reedy island and to the
marshes and plains around it. They approved the skill with
which the scattered Gallic tribe would retreat when attacked
to this river-bound island; and they made it into an " oppidum " for themselves, an " oppidum " in those times being
less a town than a stronghold in open country. The island
was an excellent and safe place for political assemblies; and
Caesar summoned the tribes to meet him there. It is almost
certain that the Gauls assembled, under the eyes of the
helmeted legionaries, on that western half of the island
where now stands the Palais de Justice. Think of that as
you enter the courtyards of the Palace to visit its lovely
Sainte Chapelle. And think when you come out of those
courts and walk again in the Boulevard du Palais that you
are crossing the site of what became the Roman forum.

With the completion of Caesar's conquest the Romans
stayed on the island for more than half a millennium, for such
a tale of centuries as stretches between, say, the fall of our
Richard II in 1399 and this present year of 1961. Caesar's
great meeting was in 53 B.C.; Clovis, king of the barbarian
but conquering Franks, made Paris his capital in A.D. 508.

They were centuries of quiet: island and hills were
embraced by the Roman peace. But within the quiet the
little oppidum became a Roman city with palace, temple,
forum, arena and baths. They called it Lutetia, a name of
romance now, but can it be that it comes from the Latin
word *luteus* meaning muddy or miry? I incline to this
belief, and it is one of my justifications for calling the
original stronghold of the Parisii a little wet island in its
marshy basin between the hills. Others have suggested a
more pleasing derivation for the name. Julian, the apostate
Roman emperor, who dearly loved Paris and often made
his home there, always wrote of it as " Louchetia," which
may come from the Greek word *leucos*, " white," and mean
the white town on its island and hill.

The journeyings of the Parisii had been over field tracks

and trestle bridges; the Romans built long well-paved roads. The original Roman road which ran, straight as a taut rope, across Lutetia, coming from Genabum (Orleans) and going on and on to Rotomagus (Rouen) is still there. You are standing on it when you stand on the Rue de la Cité and look up at Notre Dame; and, if you like, you can imagine for a moment the legions marching past you. Indeed I hope you will. You are walking straight along it (behind the legions) when you come down the Rue St. Jacques and, crossing the Petit Pont and the Pont Notre Dame, go on and on up the Rue St. Martin. Take one glance at your map and you will see it running right through Paris, over the island, north and south, and straight as the rectitude of a Roman soul.

In that long Roman quiet we need take note of only two stories, the story of a Christian saint and the story of Julian, the apostate Roman emperor. According to tradition, somewhere about A.D. 250 Dionysius came from Rome to evangelise the city and be its first bishop, bringing among other missionaries Rusticus, a priest, and Eleutherius, a deacon. On that high and holy peak to the north where once was the sacred grove of the Parisii the Romans had raised a temple to Mercury and Mars; and Dionysius, as a Christian bishop, held it his duty to desecrate this pagan place, which he attempted with the enthusiastic support of Rusticus and Eleutherius. The Roman governor, taking a different view, had all three beheaded. They were beheaded (we shall visit the spot later) about half-way up the hill, and Dionysius picked up his head and walked with it in his hands two miles and more towards the north, where he found a convert to bury him and his friends. Over his tomb rose the Abbey of St. Denis (Dionysius), the patron saint of France, and the hill on which he died with Rusticus and Eleutherius is no longer the Mount of Mercury and Mars but the Mount of the Martyrs, *Mons Martyrum*, or, as we call it, Montmartre.

The apostate Emperor was Julian, nephew of Constantine the Great, and one of the most attractive of all the Roman emperors. He was noble, just and wise, for all his renunciation of the newly established Christianity, that religion of a remote Galilean. He came to Paris and, falling in love with it like so many visitors since, made it his winter quarters during his admirable campaigns against the barbarian Germans and Franks. It is said that he built the great palace on the southern hill (later the hill of St. Geneviève), a large part of whose ruins still remain by the side of the Boulevard St. Michel, and that it was either to this palace, or to his tent, that his legionaries, so deeply attached to him, came rushing down the slope, from their camp higher up, to proclaim him Augustus (he was already Caesar) and to declare in their fervour and delight that he must accept the Empire or death at their hands. Perhaps this flattering episode increased his love for the little Lutetia. In a playful and charming book which he wrote when he was far away from Lutetia he calls it his " dear little city " and speaks of its fig trees and wines, its gentle river where the ice blocks came drifting down in winter, and its bridges of wood that lead to temple and forum on the island. In the year 363, very

The Seine, early morning

The church of St. Etienne du Mont, which holds the shrine of Sainte Geneviève

Interior of St. Etienne du Mont, showing its famous Renaissance rood screen, the only rood screen remaining in Paris

far from Paris, during a battle against the Persians in the heat of a desert, he received his mortal wound and, if the story is true, flung his lance away with the cry, " Thou hast conquered, O Galilean." *Vicisti, Galilaee.* But Montaigne says that the famous words were "Content thyself, O Nazaræan."

With this simple pattern in mind—the island and the two hills—we have culled enough basic history. We shall gather more as we go, much more, and all of it thrilling unless our souls are dead. For example, the two hills, as I have said, have long shoulders, and the left shoulder of St. Geneviève is Montparnasse while the left shoulder of Montmartre ends at Père Lachaise. The promise is great. I sometimes think that, almost unwittingly, Paris has crowned its island and two hills in gratitude to them as the source of all its life; because if you stand in any open space in Paris you see the island wearing a kind of tiara formed by the towers of Notre Dame and the spire of Sainte Chapelle, the southern hill crowned by the dome of the Panthéon, higher than anything there, and the northern hill displaying royally the white cupolas and campanile of Sacré Coeur de Montmartre, higher than anything anywhere.

2

On the Hill of St. Geneviève

2

On the Hill of St. Geneviève

O N the island there is nothing left of Rome but that
straight road between bridge and bridge, now called
the Rue de la Cité and running from the Petit Pont
to the Pont Notre Dame. To find the last traces of the
Romans you must cross from the island to the southern
hill and climb only a few yards up its slope. Cross by the
Pont St. Michel so that your few steps are up the Boulevard
St. Michel, and there, of a sudden, is Rome rising mightily
but silently before you, shoulder to shoulder with the
crowded and clattering Boul' Mich'. Those magnificent
ruins in their green garden, some of their walls sixty feet
high and two yards thick, are all that remains of a huge
Roman palace. They are so impressive on their grassy floor
that you are tempted for a moment to forget the uproarious
boulevard behind you and to imagine you are standing in
Rome itself and staring at a portion of the great Baths of
Caracalla. Baths in part these ruins are. Some have believed, as we saw, that they are part of the palace which
Julian built, but scholars now think that the real imperial
palace was on the island west of the forum and where the
Palais de Justice now stands. Did we not say that this end
of the island has always been sacred to Caesar, and the other
to God?

It is imperative that you do not remain in the boulevard
but go in and visit the great *salle* of this so-called Palais des
Thermes or " Baths of Cluny." You enter it by paying the
small fee and passing through the chambers of the Cluny
Museum which is contiguous to the ruins. The Hôtel
de Cluny is a quite lovely building in the Flamboyant

Gothic, and has been called the most beautiful piece of late medieval civil architecture in Paris; the exhibits in its various rooms are all fascinating; but what can compete with the vast and silent Roman hall into which, at the end of your passage, you descend down steps because its floor, once all tiles and mosaics, is now so many feet below the present level of Paris? Stand in the centre of that floor beneath the high-vaulted roof. There is not a sound: those thick walls of quarried stones and small red Roman bricks, built maybe at the end of the second century, keep out all the noises of today (which is saying much, for a Parisian boulevard is only a few yards distant). Wait where you stand and you will feel the silence of seventeen centuries around you.

If you look up at the ribs of the vaults you will see that they rest on corbels sculptured to represent the prows of boats; probably because the Gallo-Roman citizens of Lutetia were men of the river, sailors and traders between the winding Seine banks. Indeed, if you now cast your eyes at the fragmented column and that half-dozen of broken stones standing as exhibits by the eastern wall you will be looking at the oldest and perhaps the most wonderful relics in Paris, the parts of a votive pillar and the stones of a shrine raised by the Nautae, Lutetia's Guild of Boatmen, to Jupiter. They were discovered two and a half centuries ago beneath the choir of Notre Dame (that spot ever sacred to a god) and the inscription on the pillar shows that it was standing in place when Christ

was crucified on Golgotha. " To Jove the Great and the Good," it runs, " we, the Guild of Boatmen, founded this altar when Tiberius was Caesar."

There is one other remnant of Roman Lutetia on the hill of St. Geneviève. It is not so easy to come upon as the Palais des Thermes because it is hidden behind the high cliff-like house-blocks of the Rue Monge; nor is it so instant in its appeal as that vast Roman Frigidarium because it is not shut in with its own peace and its own past; it lies beneath a wide sky, and all too much of it is reconstruction rather than preservation. Furthermore some of it leans unromantically back against the crowded and noisy house-backs of the Rue Monge. But it is a place to sit in and think. To think till your imagination is strongly at work. For it is nothing less than the old amphitheatre of Lutetia, and they call it now Les Arènes de Lutèce.

Cut into the slope of the hill, which is the ideal way to site an amphitheatre, it was built about the same time as the Palais des Thermes, but it was not uncovered till the days of the Second Empire, in 1869, and not completely dug out of its grave till the 1880s. The simplest way to find it is to get into the long Rue Monge, which is easy enough, and then ask the first unoccupied and silent Parisian you see. He will direct you enthusiastically to an archway through the high cliff of houses; you pass through it, and find your feet on the arena floor of a great circus. Perhaps it looks small if you remember the Colosseum in Rome or the amphitheatre at Arles, but those tiers of seats sloping up behind and around you in thirty-six banks could hold sixteen thousand spectators, which must have been almost the whole population of Lutetia, there being no record of this Gallo-Roman Paris having more than twenty thousand inhabitants. Immediately before you is the theatre or stage on the level of the lowest of the tiers. A notice at another entrance, probably one of the two entrances by which the Gallo-Romans came swarming happily into their seats, states that this arena saw nautical jousts (*joutes nautiques*), gladiatorial contests, exhibitions of wild beasts, and Christian martyrdoms. One authority has even hinted at the possibility that St. Denis himself, patron saint of France, was executed here. But we shall have a very different tale to tell about that when we climb the opposite hill, Montmartre. We shall hold to the traditions of Montmartre which are centuries old.

We learn about the last of the Romans when we consider the story of St. Geneviève who has left her name on the hill. Her legend says that St. Germain l'Auxerrois, the bishop of Paris, found her as a little shepherd girl of seven years old in a village outside the city wall and was so attracted by her that he persuaded her to give her life to religion. When she was old enough she left her sheep and came to Paris and to a far wider pastoral care, because, winning the love of its citizens by her sanctity and benevolence, she rose almost at once to a position of authority which, as we peer at it in its far-away mists, straining to discern its outline, looks like a saintly feminine dictatorship. When in 451, Geneviève being still in her twenties, the terrible Attila, King of the Huns, came sweeping with his squat and Mongol-eyed horsemen out of the regions by the Caspian and across the whole of Europe, ravaging, murdering, boasting that grass would never grow again where his horses had galloped, and earning among the terrified people the name of " The Scourge of God "; and when, after many a frightful victory, he bore down upon

Paris, it was Geneviève, the beloved benefactress, who
came out of her cloister and blessed and calmed the people,
assuring them that she had the promise of God that no
harm should come to them. She organised the city's defence,
housing and helping refugees and securing siege supplies
of food; then fell to prayer. And while she prayed Attila was
hurled back by Roman and Visigoth armies at Châlons-sur-
Marne, some eighty miles from Paris.

It was Geneviève who raised the first shrine above that
burial place of St. Denis; and, most striking of all, it was she
who, after watching over her city for half a century and
more, advised its people to surrender it to Clovis now that
he had been crowned King of the Franks at Reims and converted to Christianity. Let them welcome him as King of
Paris, she counselled, and the people obeyed her because
they venerated her so. Thus Geneviève stands on one of the
divides of history, changing Paris from a Gallo-Roman to a
Frankish town; and surely this sits well in the story of Paris
which we must ever think of, with all its greatness, as a
feminine city, even as London is so patently masculine.
Geneviève met the conquering Clovis as an equal and
arranged with him this transition from an old to a new world.

Clovis, though no saint, having few scruples and less
pity, was none the less, in the grim fashion of those days, a
devoted churchman, and one day, having proclaimed Paris
the capital of France, he went out on to the summit of
Geneviève's hill and flung his battleaxe this way and that
to mark the place where a great church should arise that
would be worthy of the capital. It was to be called the
Basilica of St. Peter and St. Paul and in it he would be
buried. Before it was built Geneviève died, either in her
ninetieth year or a little earlier (the records are not clear),
and all the citizens of Paris, Gallo-Roman and Frankish
alike, bore her body in a solemn procession up the Roman
road (now the Rue St. Jacques) to the top of the hill where,
by the roadside in the Roman style, stood the Roman tombs.

Here they laid her in a spot just east and south of the tombs (which is to say east and south of the Place du Panthéon). And they left her there, to be for ever the patron saint of Paris. Over her body Clovis raised his basilica, which was still unfinished when he too came to rest there. The huge-domed Panthéon and the so-called Tower of Clovis stand now where the king's battleaxe fell. Nothing remains of his basilica. The Basilica of Saints Peter and Paul it might be officially called, but the people of Paris would have none of this; for them it was always the Church of St. Geneviève. And St. Geneviève is still an unescapable presence on the top of her hill. Her tomb may have been desecrated and emptied in the Revolution but it is still there in its golden shrine; we shall stand before it when we come into the exquisite little church of St. Etienne du Mont at the Panthéon's side.

Can it be doubted that, since it is an irrepressible human instinct to climb to the top of a hill, the old St. Geneviève ascended sometimes to the Roman tombs and turned to look back upon the island city? And is it not strange to think that her old eyes gazed down upon a walled town which was already ancient? Those thick Roman walls, either rising above a brief slope of mud and stones or sucked by the narrow-channelled river, were already five centuries old and crumbled and mouldering. Behind them rose the low-built Roman houses under their small red tiles, and among them stood the administrative palace on the west and the temple on the east. Behind these she would have descried the Roman prison on the north wall and here at the foot of the hill the fortified gateway that defended the bridge and the access on to the island. Many of these things must have seemed as romantic to her as all buildings hundreds of years old are to us.

Of course with Clovis as its king, Paris became wholly a Christian city. Was it not Clovis who when the story of

Christ's crucifixion was told to him cried indignantly,
" Would God I had been there with some of my Franks !" ?
He raised his basilica; his son, Childebert, after issuing an
edict that all relics of paganism must be overthrown (which
perhaps accounts for those broken fragments of the Nautae
pillar) raised the first cathedral of Notre Dame on the same

holy place at the island's
eastern end. It was only a
small basilica in the Roman
pattern, long and low, with
round arched windows and
a rounded apse, but it stood
there for six hundred years
till in 1163 its beautiful
daughter, with its soaring
columns and flying but-
tresses, our own Gothic
Notre Dame, began to rise
in its place—that place already sacred to worship for
a thousand years. Childe-
bert also built on the meadows of the south bank a great
abbey church which he designed for the honour of St.
Vincent whose miracle-working tunic he had brought from
Saragossa in Spain. But, as with his father's basilica, so with
this of St. Vincent; the people of Paris, regardless of its
royal founder, gave it their own name after their good
bishop, St. Germain, was buried within it. St. Germain des
Prés, St. Germain's in the Meadows, it became for them,
and so it has remained for us all ever since.

There is little more we need learn about the Frankish
city. There follow the Dark Ages and we must wait another
five centuries till Paris, like the whole of Europe, stirs in
its intellectual sleep and awakes to the Great Curiosity, to
the desire to learn the how and the why and the whence of
things; till Abélard is teaching in the precincts of Childe-

bert's Notre Dame and St. Bernard is refuting him, and
tremendous things are about to happen on the hill of St.
Geneviève.

Compared with the hill of Montmartre which is steep
and high, St. Geneviève's hill is small and easy-sloped and
low; and it may seem absurd that it should be known as
the Montagne Sainte Geneviève. But a mountain in the
history of the world it is; a very high place. It is hardly too
much to say that this small hill, crowned now by the dome
of the Panthéon, has played a greater part in Europe's
history than any other except the Acropolis rock at Athens,
crowned by the Parthenon, and the seven hills of Rome,
crowned, in ancient days, by the Capitol—or the green hill
of Golgotha.

Its greatness really began in the first years of the twelfth
century with Peter Abélard who, after teaching and disput-
ing in the Close of Notre Dame, in old monastic halls there,
decided to move out into a freer and less sternly orthodox
air, and led his hero-worshipping students in a procession
across the river to the south bank, where he taught them in
the open on the slope of the hill. Only cross (as he did) from
the very front of Notre Dame by the Pont au Double and
take a few steps into the Rue du Fouarre and you are standing
within the site of that field on which, it may fairly be said,
Abélard founded the University of Paris. Not only from
France but from England, Germany and Spain, the young
students flocked to the fame of Abélard as a teacher. He
taught, they say, as many as three thousand pupils on the
slope of the hill, with the Abbey of St. Geneviève looking
down upon him, or in the Abbey itself; but he often returned
to the island and to the precincts of Notre Dame because
here lived Héloïse in the house of her uncle, the Canon
Fulbert, and there Abélard as her tutor, some twenty
years older than she, taught her Latin, Greek, Hebrew,
Theology, Philosophy—and love. She learned to love him
with so complete and self-sacrificing a devotion that their

two names, like those of Paolo and Francesca, or Romeo and Juliet, have always been a linked symbol of romantic love.

She lived in the Rue Chanoinesse which is still there in the cathedral's shadow, though Canon Fulbert's house has long gone the same way as the dust of those old lovers.

In the years after Abélard's death and throughout the next century students from all over the world continued to pour into Paris to be taught on the sides of this hill. " Neither at Athens nor at Alexandria," says le Breton, " was there ever an influx of students such as this." The great pope, Innocent III, who contrived to make all Christendom sub-ject to his rule, said of this new University of Paris, " It is the oven where the bread of the whole world is baked." By now, in the eyes of the world, it was the New Athens. " If England," says André Maurois in his *History of France*, " has preserved in the modern world Rome's imperial and judicial tradition, Paris has played, both in letters and art, the role of Athens."

At first all the teaching was done in the open, but the students had to wear their caps and gowns as they sat on the grass in a field, or on straw in a public place. Soon some residential halls were built to house them, and at last, in 1253, Robert de Cerbon, or Sorbon, chaplain and con-fessor to France's noblest king, St. Louis, founded the first college, " The Community of Poor Masters and Scholars." Like so many of our public schools the Sorbonne was founded by a good priest for the sons of the poor and has since been appropriated, somewhat largely, by the sons of the prosperous. After the Sorbonne other colleges, repre-senting nation after nation, rose upon those slopes between the Abbey of St. Geneviève and the river. The Montagne Sainte Geneviève was now the hub and heart of the intel-lectual world; it was, as the French have always loved to say of their Paris, " *à la tête de la civilisation.*"

It is enough to mention only a few of those who studied

here and came away to divert the courses of human thought, and even, more than once, to let loose violent changes of history upon the world: Innocent III himself, Dante, St. Thomas Aquinas, St. Ignatius Loyola who founded the Jesuits, John Calvin who loosed quite a different—indeed the opposite—revolution, St. Francis Xavier, Descartes who created modern philosophy, Pascal whose writings ushered in the great classical age of French literature by shaping that most perfectly polished and tempered instrument, modern French prose, and, lastly three tremendous names: Danton, Desmoulins and Robespierre. The later phases of the Revolution and the Death of the French monarchy, thirteen centuries old, were conceived, with Danton for their father, in the womb of the Cordeliers Club towards the foot of the hill. With all of these crucial persons, great or grim, we shall have further traffic before we have finished our stories of Paris and our visits to its haunted places.

3

A Day on the Island

3

A Day on the Island

ERHAPS hardly aware that Paris had its beginning
among the reeds and willows of the island, every visitor,
guided maybe by the invisible spirits of the place, tends
to begin his pilgrimages there. And this because of three
things: Notre Dame, the Sainte Chapelle, and the Conciergerie. Probably (and maybe again guided from above) he
goes first to the cathedral. As we have seen, men began to
build this present cathedral on the site of the previous
Romanesque church in 1163, soon after the death of Abélard
and almost in the same year as the death of the Founder
and Abbess of the Convent of the Paraclete, who was
Héloïse. It was finished, almost as we see it now, in seventy
years.

If you stand in the Parvis before its western face and look
up at it, as you certainly have or will, you are standing
where the platform or stage was set up on which Henry of
Navarre, the Huguenot, was married to Marguerite de
Valois, who then went inside to attend the nuptial mass,
while her Protestant husband was left outside—on the
stage and thinking, I dare say, with a smile in his gay, mischievous eyes and at play between his sprightly moustache
and beard, that perhaps Paris, after all, was well worth a
mass. Those great twin towers and that wheel window
looked down upon the Marquise de Brinvilliers, that seven-
teenth-century lady poisoner, as she got out of the cart
which was taking her to execution and knelt with a rope
round her neck and a crucifix in her hand, to ask the compassion of Our Lady and the forgiveness of God. They
also looked down, if you believe Victor Hugo, on poor

La Sainte Chapelle and the Royal Grille before the Palais de Justice

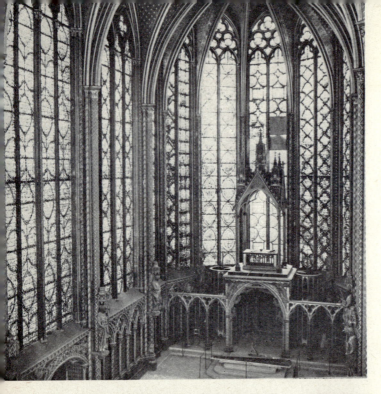

La Sainte Chapelle: upper chapel with the canopied platform on which the reliquary for the Crown of Thorns used to stand

La Sainte Chapelle: lower chapel used in former times by the servants of the King's Palace

one-eyed, hunchbacked Quasimodo, bell-ringer of Notre
Dame, as he stood and watched, captivated, the dancing of
Esmerelda the gipsy girl. From the northern tower he
sent the bad priest toppling down very justly on to the
street.

The cathedral was nearing completion in 1226 when Louis
IX, that *beau idéal* of a Christian monarch, and possibly the
noblest king that ever sat on any throne, succeeded his
father as king of France. St. Louis was then only twelve
years old, and did he as an eager boy, it is pleasant to
wonder, stand where you are standing now and gaze up
with his grave but pleased and smiling eyes at that west
front as it assumed its final shape? Those three deep-
recessed portals framed in their receding arches and
sculptured all over with scenes to teach the simple the
message of their salvation—did they then or later do their
part in guiding him into ways of righteousness? That
carven picture over the central doorway, showing the Last
Judgment, with the angel sounding the trump and the
tombs opening and the dead rising and the righteous being
separated from the wicked—had it any part in teaching
him that deep sense of fairness and justice with which he
judged his subjects in his palace on the island or under the
oak at Vincennes? That Virgin and Child between the two
doors of the north portal, the Portail de la Vierge, and the
Death and Crowning of the Virgin on the tympanum above
—had they perhaps some small part in teaching him that
almost womanly tenderness with which he would succour
the needy, shew mercy to the sinner, and regard the welfare
of his subjects (his children) as the first duty of his life after
he had paid all his duty to God? Surely he often walked
round to the back of his new cathedral—perhaps on to the
grass and reeds of that uninhabited island, now known as the
Ile Saint Louis, and there stared at the slender flying
buttresses, the gabled chapels of the apse, the pinnacles of
the transepts—stared and stared, thinking that it looked

3—P

like some enchanter's fairy-tale creation, because all this
kind of thing was new; the Gothic had only just begun
to rise, exulting, above the low, heavy, round-arched
buildings of the Romanesque.

St. Louis was a man of thirty-six when that west front
was wholly complete. Its last builders looked up at it and,
finding it so harmonious and satisfying, with its triple
entrance, wheel window, and twin towers, decided never
to erect on those towers the spires which had been designed
for them; and henceforth this type of western façade became
the pattern for other French cathedrals. Recall only
Amiens, Reims, Abbeville, and Coutances.

Notre Dame needs a book to itself, and hundreds such
have been written. But how can we in a single day, after
entering through the Portal of the Virgin into the sombre,
religious light of aisles and nave, sup properly of history's
seven hundred years that linger here? I offer one way: go
up between the round, and still almost Romanesque,
columns of the nave and beneath that high sexpartite
vaulting almost lost in the dusk above you, and, coming
to the column on the right of the choir, look up at the
famous statue of Our Lady of Paris, there on the column,
with her madonna lilies beside her, her blue curtains behind
her, and her canopy above. She is inclining a little towards
you and—yes, surely—ever so slightly smiling. She was
carved in the middle of the fourteenth century just before
the Hundred Years' War, and what has she not watched,
with that incipient smile, in more than six hundred years?
Sixty years ago Hilaire Belloc in a most learned, heartfelt,
and therefore poetical book about Paris wrote this of her
statue: " Its beauty, slight and ill-defined, is not the interest
of the statue. It is because this image dates from the awak-
ening of the capital to its position in France; because it is
the symbol of Paris . . . a kind of core and centre to the city
and, as it were, the genius, catching up the spirit of the wars
and giving to the generation of the last siege, as it will give

in the future to others in newer trials, a figure in which
all the personality of the place is stored up and remembered. . . . It received the devotion of Etienne Marcel;
it heard the outcry that followed the defeat of Poitiers and
the captivity of the king; before it was kept that great
candle, coiled as sailors coil ropes, and as long as the walls
of the city, which the Corporation vowed on the news of
that battle. It has been for these five hundred years and more
the ' middle thing ' carrying with full meaning the name of
' Our Lady of Paris ' which seems to spread out from it to
the church and to overhang like an influence the whole city
so that one might wonder sometimes as one looked at it
whether it was not the figure of Paris itself that one saw."

"It received the worship of Etienne Marcel "—that
great Provost of the Merchants who defied King and
Dauphin, established the Commune of Paris, and may be
called, perhaps, a morning star of the Revolution. It
received also, and kindly, I think, the worship of poor
François Villon, that most rascally and lovable of poets,
thief and vagrant and murderer and fugitive, who would
wander through the crooked and foul streets of fifteenth-
century Paris, now around Notre Dame, and now across
the bridge and up the southern hill—anywhere, in fact,
where mischief could be practised and profits brought away.
And much of the time as he wandered he must have been
dreaming out his ballades and roundels. *The Ballade that
Villon Made at the Request of his Mother to Invoke Our Lady:*

> *Dame du ciel, regente terrienne,*
> *Emperière des infernaulx paluz,*
> *Recevez-moy vostre humble chrestienne . . .*

Lady of Heaven and earth and therewithal
Crowned Empress of the nether clefts of Hell,
I, thy poor Christian, on thy name do call . . .
                                        (Rossetti's translation)

Mocking and melancholy, he has dreamed out for us, perhaps in the night darkness of those narrow streets, perhaps
looking up (as you now) at this kindly image of Our Lady
of Paris, surely the most famous of all songs that bewail,
though not without a wistful smile, our transience and
mortality. *The Ballade of Ladies of Bygone Days*:

> Where's Héloïse, the learned nun
> For whose sake Abeillard, I ween,
> Lost manhood and put priesthood on . . .
>
> Bertha Broadfoot, Beatrice, Alice,
> And Ermengarde the lady of Maine,
> And that good Joan whom Englishmen
> At Rouen doomed and burned her there,
> Mother of God, where are they then?
> *But where are the snows of yesteryear?*
>
> Nay, never ask this week, fair lord,
> Where they are gone, nor yet this year,
> Save with this much for an overword,
> *But where are the snows of yesteryear?*
>
> > (Rossetti's translation)

" *Mais où est le preux Charlemagne?* " he also asked in his
Ballade of Lords of Bygone Days and we in the same mood
may ask *Où est le preux Villon?* No one knows. He vanished.
He disappeared from his Paris like the snows of the previous
year. But still, across five centuries, we can but love a
miscreant who could write *The Quatrain that Villon Composed when He was Condemned to Death.* (Thank God he
escaped the municipal gallows in the Place de Grève and
the horrible gibbet of Montfaucon which stood at the corner
of the Quai de Jemmappes and of the Rue de la Grange-aux-
Belles, and which received the bodies of the criminals after
they had been hung, drawn and quartered, or broken on
rack or wheel, or boiled alive.) Ably translated by Mervyn
Savill the excellent quatrain runs:

I am François, wretched clown,
Born in Paris near Ponthoise town.
My neck in a noose swinging to and fro
Will feel the weight of my arse below.

The sentence of death was commuted to imprisonment for
life and after four years he was set free, to disappear into
the mists one day.

You will certainly attend one service in Notre Dame,
and perhaps if your French is not good enough to follow
the sermon fully, or if the sermon is not potent enough
to hold your attention and convince you of sin, you may
find yourself looking around at the wonderful fane in which
you are seated and sinking deep into thoughts of your own.
Should this lapse happen to you, I would suggest the
following course for your meditations. You will have time
for it because the sermon will be long. Only a few yards
from you, westward across the island, is the Palais de
Justice, whose vast hall, once the celebrated Grand Salle,
has now the lovely name of the Salle des Pas Perdus, the
Hall of the Lost Footsteps. Sad and fitting name enough
for that place, but how apt also it would be to think of this
vast nave in which you are sitting as The Nave of the Lost
Footsteps. Let that be the text of your meditations now.
What are some of the footsteps it has heard; some of the
sights it has seen?

It heard the steps of St. Louis when each year on Holy
Thursday he came in to wash the feet of the poor men.
It heard those of our Henry V after his conquest of France
and his acceptance as King of France and England;
it saw the coronation of his young son, our Henry VI;
it heard the *Te Deum* of Henry of Navarre after *his* conquest of Paris (he is inside the cathedral now); it saw
the ceremonies of the Relevailles, those churchings of
Marie Antoinette after the births of her doomed Bourbon
children, while the guns boomed their salute without, but
the streets were silent in their gathering hostility to this

Austrian queen on Revolution's eve; it saw the sacrilegious feast of the Goddess of Reason during the Revolution when a dancer from the Opera played the leading role, taking the place of Christ upon that altar yonder, and all the people danced before her—footsteps indeed! It saw the storing and stocking of the wine-casks when the dishonoured House of God was turned into a wine store—more strange footsteps—and the Ceremony of Atonement when, under Napoleon, the church was given back to Our Lady of Paris; it saw the Coronation of Napoleon and Josephine, and the *Te Deum*, after Napoleon's defeat, for the Restoration of the Monarchy. Lastly, in our own day, in 1944, after hearing many gun-shots in the Parvis without, where many fell fighting for the liberation of their city, as we shall later learn, it heard the footsteps of General de Gaulle and of the Leaders of the Resistance who had come to sing *Magnificat* before the altar of their liberated city. "My soul doth magnify the Lord."

Maybe this will be enough to dwell upon in the jewelled dusk of Notre Dame.

One cannot speak of St. Louis without the words "Sainte Chapelle" coming into mind and bringing with them a sense of remembered wonder and delight. St. Louis loved Paris, a love which has always been mutual. He loved the island too and chose to live there rather than in the new Louvre on the northern shore. For this purpose he rebuilt the Palace where you may still see a few traces of his work; but what most matters to us now is that he built the Sainte Chapelle. There in the court of what was his palace it stands today, almost exactly as he left it; and, standing there, it seems to keep the spirit of this saintly king for ever in the exact centre of his capital. He built it "to the glory of God and France" as a shrine for the Crown of Thorns and other relics of the Passion: the Holy Lance (a piece of rusted steel), the Sacred Nail, and a fragment of the Cross.

The Crown of Thorns he had acquired from Baldwin, Emperor of Constantinople, and he sent two chosen friars to weigh out the price in gold and bring the precious relic back. They brought it to Sens where the King went to meet it; and from Sens he and his brothers, walking barefoot, carried it in its reliquary on their shoulders to Paris and Notre Dame. The people crowded into their new cathedral, then white against the sky, to kneel before it and wonder at it and, let us hope, purpose amendment for the future. After this, Louis and his brothers, followed by their half-English mother, Blanche of Castille, carried it into their Palace church till the Sainte Chapelle should be ready for it, a casket of soaring stones and dazzling glass.

You may see much of their story illustrated in the dazzling glass when you come into its " upper chapel " which is the Sainte Chapelle we remember; the rather low-roofed " lower chapel " by which we enter was but the chapel for the King's servants. We climb to this upper chapel by a winding stone stairway, past stone walls and arrow-slit windows that tell us it was built in the age of castles, and we issue from this cold little tower into a blaze of gilt and colour, and into the heart of the middle ages.

The slender clustered columns sweep up like water-jets

to the sprays of the vaulted roof; the walls between them
are tall window-mosaics of richly stained glass in which
are depicted more than a thousand scenes from Bible stories
and a serial record of the translation of the Crown of
Thorns from Constantinople to Notre Dame and to the
Palace. There, if you can find them among the glowing
lozenges of colour, you can see the two friars weighing out
the gold; St. Louis and his brothers bearing the reliquary
barefoot to Paris; and Queen Blanche following behind with
a tall candle in her hand. At first you may think the colours
are too rich, too brilliant, too much of a good thing, especially the astonishing blues, but remember you are standing
in the Middle Ages and this was how they loved colour and
how they liked to illuminate with fearless richness all sacred
things. Only remember our Book of Kells.

Three things in this Sainte Chapelle, this incomparable
chef-d'oeuvre of the thirteenth century, you must contemplate
for more than a little while. The deep recesses or niches
both left and right, under the windows of the fourth bay,
were the places reserved for the King and his family. Just
beyond the niche on the right is a kind of " leper-squint "
or small slanted window through which the altar could be
watched from an unseen place outside; this place was the
oratory of St. Louis where sometimes he preferred to worship alone and unseen. In the centre of the apse is the high
gilded platform, with an ogival baldachin above it, on which
the holy relics would be exposed; two winding stairways
in little open turrets lead up to it, and the one on the left
is still the original one up which St. Louis would climb to
his royal task of opening the reliquary.

The Sainte Chapelle was finished and ready for the relics
in 1248, and into it, for its First Mass and its Consecration,
came St. Louis with his court and some of his crusaders.
Since he was just about to set forth on a crusade, the
seventh, I think that, while we may picture him in the
vermilion surcoat, ermine trimmed, which he wore on

state occasions, those of his courtiers and people who had
" taken the cross " wore—proudly, I am sure—their cloaks
with the cross on the shoulder. I must suspect too that they
abstracted themselves from prayer at times to gaze up at
the stone-vaulted roof, at the soaring seven-windowed apse,
and round about them at the clustered pillars and the lofty
windows all glowing with coloured stories for their comfort
and improvement.

You come out of the Sainte Chapelle courtyard, and you
are in the Boulevard du Palais. Remind yourself again that
you are now probably standing in the midst of what was
once the Roman forum; indeed disperse nineteen hundred
years and see for a moment Caesar walking there. Then
look at the fine tall wrought-iron grille that screens the
forecourt of the Palace, the Cour du Mai, so called because
the Corporation of the Clerks of the Court used to plant
a tree there on the first of May and celebrate around it.
This very handsome railing has three gates in it, and the
central or great gate is surmounted by a crowned globe ornamented with the *fleur-de-lis,* the emblem since Clovis of the
Kings of France. Truly a *grille royale.* And yet it was only
completed in 1785 after a great fire at the palace and thus
was almost contemporary with the unique, and in very
truth " world-shaking " scene which you are about to
recreate. It might almost have been raised as a richly gilt
but ironic décor for it, because the scene was enacted at
about ten o'clock on October 16th, 1793.

In the far right-hand corner of the court, by the side of
the broad flights of stairs you can see a round archway. From
it eight steps descend to a narrow court below. The archway
is open now but in 1793 it enclosed a barrier of iron bars
with an iron wicket in the middle of them, because those
steps led down to the door of the Palace prison, the Conciergerie. During the Revolution more than two thousand
prisoners came up those steps and under that arch, their

hands bound behind them, and climbed into the waiting
tumbrils which would take them to the guillotine.

On this day a single prisoner is to come to that high-
wheeled two-horse tumbril waiting in the forecourt near
the iron barrier. All the city knows what is happening
because the streets have been noisy for some time with the
beating of drums, the marching of soldiers, and the ringing
of horse-hooves when mounted men have gone cantering
by. Thirty thousand soldiers have taken up their positions
along the roads and in the squares or are even now marching
into the Place de la Révolution (the Place de la Concorde).
Detachments of infantry and cavalry are within this Cour du
Mai, and an excited multitude of watchers, some of whom,
however, look horrified and glum, is pressed against the
royal grille.

Now at last a posse of soldiers comes up the steps, and
behind them a woman with hands bound behind her and the
executioner at her side holding the end of the rope as one
holds a dog-leash. She wears a long white muslin gown,
new and clean as if donned for an occasion of some importance, and her hair which has been partly hacked away is
covered by a kind of white mob-cap, frilled. Actually it is a
widow's cap from which she has removed the black
mourning scarf. Head carried contemptuously, she comes
to the cart and mounts it with her linked and silent com-
panion. She takes one look at the priest who is seated in
the cart, and turns from him, not to look his way again
because in her eyes he is a renegade from the Catholic
Church, a " constitutional priest " who has succumbed to
the terms of the Revolution; he is in civilian clothes. The
husband of this prisoner went to the guillotine nine months
before her under the name of " Louis Capet," so she is
known now merely as " The Widow Capet " but he was
in fact Louis XVI of France, and she was his queen, Marie
Antoinette.

That narrow court below the archway, and the entrance

to the Galerie des Prisonniers with its reception office
where the prisoners were " signed for " or " signed out "
are now a refreshment-room where barristers and clerks
and visitors to the Palais—and you too, if you wish—can
take a light lunch on the spot where the bound Queen of
France went by.

Here, exactly as it was " entered up " and " filled in " at
five o'clock this morning, is the Requisition sent to the
Commandant General of the armed forces of the city, for
the soldiers required today. The words not in italics are
those " filled in " in the vacant spaces.

AU NOM DE LA REPUBLIQUE

*L'Accusateur Public, près le Tribunal criminel-révolutionnaire établi
à Paris par la loi du 10 Mars 1793, en exécution du jugement du
Tribunal* de aujourdhuy *requiert le citoyen commandant-général de la
force armée parisienne, de prêter mainforte et mettre sur pied la force
publique, nécessaire a l'exécution dudit jugement rendu contre* Marie
Antoinette Lorraine, autriche Veuve de Louis Capet *et qui la
condamne à la peine de* Mort *laquelle exécution aura lieu aujourdhuy
à* Dix *heures du Matin sur la place publique de* La Révolution *de
cette ville. Le citoyen commandant-général est requis d'envoyer ladite
force publique, cour du Palais, ledit jour à* huit *heures precises du*
Matin.

Fait à Paris, le 25 *du* 1er *mois de l'an* second *de la République
française, une et indivisible.*

It is signed with a flourish by Fouquier-Tinville, the
Public Prosecutor, who many months later will go the
same way to the guillotine as he has sent the Widow Capet.

Of the three gates in the handsome railing it is the one
on the left, as we stand in the Boulevard du Palais, through
which her tumbril comes, escorted by the mounted and the
foot soldiers. There is no pavement in this far-off day nor
indeed any Boulevard du Palais; only the narrow Rue de la

Barillerie, and the jolting cart jerks over a gutter as it turns northward towards the river. The great windows of the Hall of the Lost Footsteps look down upon it as it goes on. The crowd, so far as it can, follows after it; and we will follow too, but only as far as the quay. We shall see more of the Queen's last journey when we stand in the Rue St. Honoré and on the steps of St. Roch, and in the Place de la Concorde.

Meanwhile we turn westward along the Quai de l'Horloge to enter the Conciergerie Prison, where we shall find many traces of the first Capets who reigned in the twelfth and thirteenth centuries, but shall forget them all when we see the grim little cell in which the widow of that name dressed herself for her last journey. This part of the Palace is called the Conciergerie because it was once the residence and charge of the Concierge, or Chief of the Jurisdiction known as the Bailliage du Palais, which we may translate perhaps as the Bailiwick of the Palace.

We enter the Conciergerie through the two round, cone-capped thirteenth-century towers, the Tour César and the Tour d'Argent, and crossing the little Cour d'Entrée come to a door on its right. Passing through this, after paying our fee, we go down a few steps which, as nothing else in Paris can, lead us down one hundred and seventy years into the darkness of the Revolution. We find ourselves in the Salle des Gardes, a large grey vaulted chamber with massive pillars dividing it into two naves. They used to call it the

Great Guard Room of St. Louis, but this was wrong because it is the work of the next century, the fourteenth. It is rather dark down here; no noise from quay or river penetrates the stout ancient walls; nothing anywhere belongs to our day; so it is not difficult to leave the twentieth and nineteenth centuries behind.

You go from this Salle des Gardes into a long broad corridor which from the iron grille on your left you can see was once a part of the vast Salle des Gens d'Armes, another magnificent Gothic hall. This corridor or separated portion of the hall, in which we now are, was named in the Revolution the Rue de Paris, and in it the prisoners awaiting their fate were stacked by the hundred, lying, if there was any room to lie, on straw. Some sighed, some cursed, some prayed, and some were just terribly silent as they lay on this stone floor or leaned against that stone wall. You have seen many a reproduction of this high stony windowless place in plays and films of the Revolution. It should be remembered that it and the Salle des Gens d'Armes are exactly beneath the Hall of the Lost Footsteps; what a hall of lost footsteps we have here.

Indeed we are now in the very heart and burning focus of the Revolution, for above the Salle des Gardes from which we have come is the Première Chambre Civile. This, though greatly changed now, was the justice hall of the Revolutionary Tribunal which heard the sentence of death pronounced on nearly all the most famous victims of the guillotine, including the Widow Capet. It heard the great voice and the great laugh of Danton, who cried out, possibly loud enough to be heard down here, when Fouquier-Tinville, the prosecutor, formally asked his name and abode, " My name is Danton, a name tolerably well known in the Revolution; my abode will soon be Nothingness; but I shall be living in the Panthéon of History." It is possible that our guide has indicated to us an opening in the wall which reveals a winding stone staircase. This led up to the

Revolutionary Tribunal; prisoners went winding up it to their trial, and for the most part came down it condemned.

The Rue de Paris is long and dim, and we come out of it into a narrow and yet dimmer cross-wise passage, which is the Galerie des Prisonniers. A few steps to the right and we are at the entrance into the Queen's cell. Nowadays it is as much the central core of this grim building as is the little burial vault in the heart of the Great Pyramid. It is a narrow cell with thick walls, a groined vault, a brick floor and a window now leaded and filled with coloured glass.

You will wish to picture Marie Antoinette here in her last days and her last hours—Marie Antoinette whose Grand Apartments once included the Grande Galerie des Glaces at Versailles, probably the finest room in the world, and her Private Apartments the beautiful little Salon de la Reine in the Trianon. It is important, therefore, to realise exactly what it was like in that distant month of October 1793; some of the guide books are misleading.

As we stand in it there is an opening on our right into a parallel and similar cell, from which again there is an opening into the large room known as the Chapelle des Girondins.

But documents, plans and engravings in the Musée Carnavalet show that, when the Queen was here, the doorway by which we entered was a blank wall with a little window in it looking out on to the Galerie des Prisonniers. Against this wall stood the head of the Queen's bed. The cell was entered by a door in the side wall opposite the foot of the bed. Beyond this doorway, in a similar cell, the gendarmes sat whose duty it was to keep watch over the Queen; and only a screen stood between them and her when she undressed or lay in the bed. Other than the bed there was no furniture except a table, a chair and a candle-stick.

There was no communication, as there is now, with the opposite cell on the right, which was the cell to which Robespierre was carried, bleeding and in an agony from his shot jaw, on the dreadful night of the 9th–10th Thermidor (July 27th–28th, 1794), to await his journey to the guillotine when daylight and afternoon came. Is it not strange and fascinating to think that Robespierre came to the cell which was side by side with the Queen's? Let the Queen be the regal representative of all the host of the Revolution's victims; Robespierre our natural and elected representative of the Revolution itself.

Neither was there any communication in those days between Robespierre's cell and the Chapelle beyond.

The present window in the Queen's cell is larger than it was then, but the encircled panes in the coloured glass give us the dimensions of the small round window through which she must often have looked out at the daylight in the Cour des Femmes.

It is thought that the Queen received the Sacrament kneeling in this cell. At some date early in the next century Charles Etienne Magnin, then the Curé of St. Germain l'Auxerrois, wrote the following story; and I can see little reason to doubt it, despite some wild, sad words of the Queen which we shall read. The Abbé Magnin was one of the clergy of St. Roch when the Queen was incarcerated in the Conciergerie.

" I declare that the Sieur Brault, the successor of Rictad at the Conciergerie, and well known to Mademoiselle Fouché when he was concierge at the prison of La Force, granted her insistent requests. The door of the (Queen's) cell was opened to her. The presence of one so devout sweetened for a little the situation of the Queen, and by her efforts and solicitations I obtained from this new warden the happiness of presenting myself to Her Majesty.

" The memory of what had passed when the King was in the same cruel position persuaded me to propose to the Queen that I should say Mass in the obscure lodging (*réduit obscur*) which she occupied and should give her the Holy Communion. I assured Her Majesty that it would be easy for us to bring all the objects necessary for these august ceremonies.

" We had, in effect, at our disposition in these dreadful days some very small chalices and missals and some portable altar stones only a little larger than the foot of one of the little chalices. All these articles would go into a work-bag (*sac à ouvrages*) and we could easily hide them in our pockets.

" The Queen, understanding this, accepted and thanked us.

" Among the gendarmes who were employed as the cell's special guard we had remarked two who, by their profound respect for their Sovereign, and the free manifestations of their religious sentiments, had inspired us with great confidence. I did not hesitate to tell them of the happiness which the Queen was about to enjoy.

" These Frenchmen, good and faithful Christians, testified to their desire to participate in it. The day was fixed and the concierge came to take us during the night to a place indicated, and he conducted us into the prison.

" I heard the Queen's confession. Mademoiselle Fouché had prepared herself to receive her Lord, and the gendarmes assured me that they ardently desired to communicate in a circumstance so fortunate for them. We prepared on the table, without losing a moment, all that was necessary. I celebrated the august Sacrifice of our altars and I gave the Communion to the Queen who received from her God the courage to support without murmuring all the torments to which she was destined. Mademoiselle Fouché and the two gendarmes were admitted at the same time to this Divine Banquet.

" The need to be brief does not permit me to paint the emotion stirred in me by this scene so touching, which took place in those first days of the month of October 1793."

It is now half-past four in the morning of October 16th, 1793, and the Queen has just come down the stone stairway

A Bateau Mouche on the Seine near the Palais de Justice

The Seine from the flèche of Notre Dame

Notre Dame from
a Bateau Mouche

from hearing her condemnation in the Tribunal above. She
sits wearily at the little table in this cell and asks one of her
jailers for paper and a pen. He gives them to her and is
moved enough to bring her a second candlestick. Between
the flames of the two candles she begins to write a letter to
Madame Elisabeth, the King's sister—Madame Elisabeth
who, though the Queen does not know this, and cannot
apparently imagine it, will in due time come to this prison
and follow her to the scaffold. She sits writing this letter
while Fouquier-Tinville, in his office in the Tour Bonbec
(the third of the grim Conciergerie towers) is filling up
that Requisition for the city's armed force.

" October 16th at half-past four in the morning.

" It is to you, Sister that I am writing for the last time.
I have just been sentenced to death, but not to a shameful
one, since this death is only shameful to criminals . . . I am
calm, as one may well be when one's conscience is clear,
though deeply grieved at having to forsake my poor
children . . . Through you I send them both my blessing,
in the hope that some day, when they are older, they will
be with you once more and able to enjoy your tender care . . .
I die in the Catholic, Apostolic, and Roman religion, in
that of my fathers, that in which I was brought up and which
I have always professed. Having no hope of any spiritual
consolation, not even knowing whether there are still
priests of this religion in France, and feeling that should
there be such I should expose them to great risks were they
to visit me here, I sincerely ask God's forgiveness for all
the faults I have committed since I was born. I trust that,
in His goodness, He will hear my last prayers, as well as
those which I have long been making that, in His pity and
goodness, He may receive my soul.

" I ask the forgiveness of all those whom I have known,
and especially of you, my sister, for the sorrow which,
unwittingly, I may have caused them. I forgive my enemies
the evil they have done me. . . ."

4—P

There is more of it; but that will do. The writing of the letter must have taken a long time, and it is likely that, before it was finished, the dawn was coming in through that small round window and paling the flames of the candles. She was now weeping quietly, probably moved to tears as one often is by one's own words. Worn out, benumbed, and in the awful peace of despair, she lay on the bed in the breaking dawn and heard, no doubt, the distant beating of the drums in the Paris " Sections " that were summoning the thirty thousand soldiers for her last royal procession.

Later the kitchen maid of the Governor's wife, an illiterate peasant girl, Rosalie Larmorlière, who had been detailed to look after her throughout her seventy-six days in the Conciergerie, came and begged her to take a little of the soup which she had made for her. The Queen gently declined it, saying, " Child, I want nothing more. For me everything is finished."

But Rosalie was persistent and the Queen yielded, surely because she didn't want to disappoint the child.

It is to Rosalie that we owe most of these details of the Queen's last hours in this cell.

The Queen took only a few spoonfuls, and soon after that she began to dress for the scaffold. Because the gendarme guarding her for death had been ordered not to leave the cell, she asked Rosalie to stand between her and him, as she removed the black mourning which she had worn before the Tribunal. They had forbidden her to wear it in the tumbril lest it angered the people—or, I suspect, lest it stirred their sympathy. Instead she put on the long white gown, drawn in at the waist, and the frilled cap after removing from it the widow's scarf. I have no warrant for suggesting, but I do it with some confidence, that she had about her person somewhere the yellow glove which had belonged to her little son, the Dauphin, or at least the lock of his hair which she had kept in her bosom ever since he was reft from her. She drew on her best shoes for her steps up the scaffold.

Then waited. Listening to the noises of the bright day that now surged up against the walls of the prison. At last, when it was nearly ten o'clock, Sanson, the executioner, very tall and young and dreadful, came in. He cut her hair for the axe, and took her hands to bind them, at which she asked, " Must you bind my hands? The King's were not bound." But she submitted, and was led out of the cell and along the Galerie des Prisonniers to the Cour du Mai— escorted out on the end of that slackened leash. With her went a thousand years of the French monarchy.

Besides the Queen's cell there are three other places you must see down here in this dismal grey bowel of the Conciergerie. Just outside the Queen's cell, only a few paces along the Galerie des Prisonniers, and along the way to the tumbrils that she trod, is a dark little recess behind an iron grille. It is no more than a windowless hovel, or lightless cage, with a bench against the wall. It is the place where they shut behind bars those who were due for the next tumbril. Here the condemned waited, their hair hacked short and their hands bound behind them. What thoughts this small hovel must have held. Among women who sat on that bench were Madame Elisabeth, and the lovely young wife of Camille Desmoulins, and Charlotte Corday, of whom we must speak later. Though it is possible that these dark walls only saw Charlotte Corday standing proudly.

Then there is the Salle, or Chapelle, des Girondins which you enter by passing through the Queen's cell and Robespierre's. This large arched chamber with its elliptical apse was the ancient chapel of the Conciergerie but was used as a large communal cell when the Revolution was crowding the prison with as many as twelve hundred prisoners. To this room, for their last night alive, and to-wards midnight, came the twenty-one Girondins singing the Marseillaise along the Galerie des Prisonniers.

The Girondins, a loosely connected party in the Legisla-tive Assembly and the National Convention, were so called because their most prominent and eloquent leaders were deputies from the Department of the Gironde in south-western France. Prime movers of the Revolution at first, they had become disgusted with its savageries, denounced them, and in consequence had been treated as reactionaries, arrested in large numbers, and condemned. Twenty-two of them had been sentenced at about ten o'clock on this night, but one of them, Valazé, had immediately stabbed himself to death, so only twenty-one came singing along that dark corridor. It was the night of October 30th, 1793, just fourteen days after the Queen went along the corridor, the opposite way, to her tumbril. The body of Valazé was borne along behind them, to share their night in this old chapel. They spent the night here singing and jesting and, as far as might be, feasting and carousing—with Valazé's body lying on the floor beside them. Carlyle calls it the Last Supper of the Girondins. Vergniaud, perhaps their greatest and most eloquent leader, presided over the meal. He had poison enough for himself but not enough for his companions, so he refused to take it, preferring to die with

them. Once the Presi-dent of the Legislative Assembly, he now took the chair at this assem-bly, and presided over the eloquence, laughter and singing.

Next morning the twenty-one went to the guillotine, shouting " Vive la République "

and singing their Marseillaise. Valazé's body travelled with
them to be guillotined too.

Among the exhibits in this room is a picture of them
seated at their table for this last banquet, and you will see
that the room in the picture is hardly any different from
what it is now. Other exhibits are a facsimile of a letter
which the Queen, having no pen, pricked out with a pin;
a facsimile of her last letter quoted above, with the blots
on it that may be the print of her tears; a knife from the
guillotine; and a picture which you must notice of twelve
men in a tumbril going to the guillotine. One of those
facing you is André Chénier, the young poet, sometimes
called the Keats of France.

We pass out of the Salle des Girondins into the Cour
des Femmes, the courtyard where the women prisoners
took their exercise and washed their linen at a fountain
still there. It is an oblong yard enclosed by the grey walls
of the prison. A high spiked railing cuts off its south-
eastern corner, making of it a small triangular space on
which barred windows look down. This was the area
reserved for men. The bell on the wall between two dark
arches is the one that told the prisoners their tumbrils
were ready. The Cour des Femmes is almost exactly the
same today as it was then; so the eyes of Marie Antoinette,
Danton, Desmoulins, Charlotte Corday, André Chénier, the
Girondins, and later Marshal Ney, saw it as we see it now.
Some of these took a last look at it, as at their last earthly
home, when the bell summoned them to the tumbrils.

Even more terrible to think of, there occurred in this
place the massacre of September 2nd and 3rd, 1792, when
Maillard and his cut-throat gangs, encouraged by the
Assembly, went from prison to prison, to l'Abbaye, La
Force, Châtelet, Bicêtre, Salpetrière, Conciergerie, in order
to slaughter all whom they deemed to be traitors, or likely
traitors, to the Revolution. Two hundred and more were
murdered in the Conciergerie. Long ago you used to be

able to see in the Bibliothèque de la Conciergerie the vellum-bound folio which lay open on Maillard's desk, with the names of the prisoners who were to be summarily killed. Its pages were stained with blood imprinted by the fingers of his assassins who, having despatched several victims, had turned its pages to find the names of more. You could also see in a drawer the receipts for twenty-four francs, the fee paid for every murder.

Note this terrible name of Maillard. We are due to encounter it again on a slope of St. Geneviève's hill. But here let us leave the Conciergerie, returning by the silent Rue de Paris and Salle des Gardes, out of the eighteenth century and issuing into the bright Paris of today.

4

Haunted Places on the Hill

4

Haunted Places on the Hill

FROM the slopes of St. Geneviève's hill, as we have implied, came that main stream which, gathering all tributaries to itself, swelled into the great and turbulent torrent we call the French Revolution; a torrent which was to irrigate all the old dry places of the world, and whose force is far from spent today. Desmoulins, Danton and Robespierre were all children of the University: Desmoulins and Robespierre had sat side by side on the benches of the Jesuit College; Danton came from his peasant home in Champagne to study law at the University and, falling in love with Paris (after the fashion of the Emperor Julian and all the rest of us) made his home here on the flank of the hill and founded nearby his club of the Cordeliers. It was called the Cordeliers because it held its meetings in the old convent of the Cordeliers, as the French named the Franciscans because of the white knotted cord they wore. Desmoulins, Robespierre, Marat, Hébert all became members of Danton's club, and there they plotted the Revolution and the Republic. Thus, after six hundred years of having the University on its breast, this little hill was delivered of a monstrous progeny.

If you will walk with me from the Panthéon, the hill's summit and the University's heart, a little way westward to the Rue de l'Ancienne Comédie (it is on the north side of the Boulevard St. Germain, a hundred yards or so eastward of the great church of St. Germain des Prés) and if you will pause there at its mouth and look about you, you will be looking at some of the seed-beds of the Revolution; it is astonishing what you can see and learn, and imaginatively re-create, from this one vantage-point, and all within a radius of about a hundred yards.

Opposite you, across the boulevard, stands the huge statue of Danton with his famous words inscribed upon it, " *Pour vaincre les ennemis de la Patrie il nous faut de l'audace, encore de l'audace, et toujours de l'audace.*" It stands almost on the site of his house, where he was arrested to take the final consequences of " *l'audace* " and die five days later on the guillotine to which he had sent so many others. Weary of too much bloodshed, he was ready to go. " *C'est bien,*" he said. " I prefer now to be guillotined rather than to guillotine. Besides, mankind bores me. March the thirty-first: it was about this season of the year that I set up the Revolutionary Tribunal; I ask forgiveness of God and man."

To the left of Danton's statue there used to be, till the Germans shop-lifted it, a statue of Broca; and it covered almost the exact site of the house in which Charlotte Corday stabbed Marat to the heart as he sat in his slipper bath. He had to take frequently to this medicated bath and sit at work in it because of a skin disease from which he suffered. You must understand that these houses are not there now because the wide Boulevard St. Germain was driven right through them. But imagine his door there. On a day of torrid July heat in 1793 Charlotte descended at this door from a fiacre and asked his " washerwoman " if she could see Citoyen Marat because she " came with something that would touch his heart." She could put it into his power, she said " to do France a great service." She was admitted at length to his presence where he sat in the breast-high bath, writing on a stool at his side, and as soon as she could she uncovered the sheath knife which she had bought in the Palais Royal and drove it powerfully home.

Marat's house was only a little way from the Cordeliers' Club which was in the Rue de l'Ecole de Médecine, there before you—on the left across the boulevard.

Now observe, by your left shoulder as you stand here,

an old archway leading into a narrow cobbled court. The house that flanks the archway on its left, No. 21 Rue de l'Ancienne Comédie, was—can you believe it?—the home of Dr. Guillotin. And in a house behind it, and so within the old cobbled court, the doctor experimented on rats and sheep with his machine for speedy and humane decapitations. Before you pass into the little court, which is all that is left of the old Cour du Commerce, glance at No. 14 on the opposite side of the street.

There for a hundred years, from 1689 to 1782, the Comédie Française had its home till it moved to the theatre in the Tuileries. This accounts for the street's name. It probably accounts also for the Café Procope at No. 13, almost directly opposite the old theatre. The café came here in 1689 and claims to be the oldest café in the world, no more and no less. The inscription on its wall says, " Here Procopio dei Coltelli founded in 1686 (*sic*) the oldest café in the world and the most celebrated centre of the literary and philosophical life in the eighteenth and nineteenth centuries. It was frequented by La Fontaine, Voltaire, the Encyclopaedists, Franklin, Danton, Marat, Robespierre, Napoleon, Victor Hugo, Balzac, Gambetta, Verlaine and Anatole France." Danton and Marat, you observe, who lived so near. We may say, I think, that the Old Comedy left this district in 1782 and less than ten years later the New Tragedy was in occupation. It was in the Café Procope that Citoyen Jullian introduced the red Phrygian cap, or *bonnet rouge,* shaped like the half of an egg, which was to be the symbol of Revolution and Liberty because among the Romans such a cap used to be placed on the heads of slaves set free.

Now go through the archway into the Cour du Commerce. It is small and narrow and cobbled, but the long, low building on the eastern side, facing the site of Dr. Guillotin's experimental laboratory, is the actual place where Marat printed his raging and inflammatory journal, *L'Ami du Peuple,* which by its aspersions, invectives, and denunciations, provided so many patients for the doctor's death-machine. You will see that, a hundred and sixty years later, it is still an Imprimerie.

Walk a few steps along the cobbles northward and turn into the Cour de Rouen, or Rohan, as they spell it here. Where but in old Paris would you find a little court within a little court? Why, you pass out of this second court into a third, a tiny, gated affair. Before you leave it, turn and look up at the tall and once dignified but now decaying house with the three roof-windows, each crowned by a different pediment. This is the once elegant home which King Henry II built for the lady who had been the mistress of his father, François I, and was now his mistress. Into this secluded and quiet court the King would come for his hours of dalliance with that ageing but practised concubine and comforter, Diane de Poitiers. We are back in ancient comedy now, and as I look up at that neat little mansion with its slender, aristocratic windows, I wonder if the poor and unfashionable people who live there today know its story.

In writing this book it has seemed best to me that, while touching upon the great sights of Paris which guide books expound in detail, I should pay a larger attention to places of deep interest which guide books seldom mention. And inevitably these will be places which have always exercised an enormous fascination on me.

One of the heroes of my youth was Condorcet, that brilliant mathematician, philosopher, encyclopaedist, statesman and idealist who, becoming horrified like the Girondins by the excesses of his fellow revolutionaries, denounced them and was accordingly declared an enemy of the Republic and placed "outside the law." What this would have meant in the end was shown by the execution of the Girondins, whose arrest he had loyally denounced; so friends who loved him sought for him some place where he could be hidden.

Quitting the Cour de Rouen, cross the wide Boulevard St. Germain (taking your life in your hands) and come by the Rue de Condé to the Rue de Vaugirard. It holds for us places of overwhelming interest. A brief walk along it brings you to the mouth of a side-street, the Rue Servandoni. A narrow artery, curving between high old houses towards a glimpse of St. Sulpice, it is just such a Paris street, with its épiceries, bistrots, and boucheries, as Utrillo should have painted, giving it the light and the colours that never were on sea or land. Go down it only as far as No. 15. No. 15 is now divided and its ground floor is occupied by both a small épicerie and a small bookshop. But look up and you will see that it was once quite a handsome home. You will see also a plaque saying, " *En 1793 & 1794 Condorcet, proscrit, trouva un asile dans cette maison.*"

In 1793 a Madame Vernet lived here, and she willingly consented to take him into her house and hide him. Though not even knowing his name, she said, " If he is virtuous and just, as you say, Messieurs, let him come and come quickly, for even while we are talking he may be taken." She hid him either in a top room, or in a little chamber up a flight of steps in her court at the back. Here, proscribed, dishonoured, and in fear of a criminal's death, he wrote his greatest work, *L'Esquisse d'un Tableau historique des Progrès de l'Esprit Humain*," an outline of the slow, steady progress of the Spirit of Man towards perfection.

When the Girondins were executed he went to Madame Vernet and insisted that his presence in her home was a danger to her life and he must go. She replied, " The Convention, Monsieur, has the right to put you outside the law; it has not the power to put you outside humanity. You will stay." *Vous resterez*. He stayed and wrote, but after a time, suspecting that the house was watched, he slipped from it, unseen by Madame Vernet, and hid for days and nights in stone quarries and woods. Then he was arrested on suspicion and flung into a cell, where his jailers in the morning found him dead on the floor. It is disputed whether he died from exhaustion or from taking some poison concealed in a ring on his hand.

Lamartine, in his *Histoire des Girondins,* states that Condorcet " shut himself up with some books and his thoughts in a room high up on the top floor of Madame Vernet's house." Perhaps. But Monsieur the épicier maintains that the little lonely chamber up the steps in the back court, which is completely screened from the road, was the hiding place, and he will show it to you. I like to think that he has the truth of it, but what is certain is that it was in a room on the ground floor near the street, which surely means a room that is now either the grocer's shop or the bookshop, that those magnificent words were spoken, *Vous resterez*. Certain too that it was from that quite handsome doorway at the side that Condorcet slipped away.

Opposite the Ecole des Beaux Arts, across the Rue Bonaparte, is the Rue des Beaux Arts. Here on a winter's day in 1900, in No. 13 which is still the same small Hôtel d'Alsace, Oscar Wilde lay dying in poverty and almost at the charges of the kindly hotel-keeper. " I have always lived beyond my means," said this High Priest of *beaux arts*, "and now I am dying beyond them." The room in which he died is No. 11 on the first floor overlooking the garden. A great mirror on the north wall has always been there, one of those vast wall-mirrors for which he used to say the Victorians should never be forgiven; it pictured him dying in the very arms of his landlord, with his friends, Robert Ross and Reginald Turner, standing by. It pictured him lying dead.

Now to the place which, for me, is the most moving of all on this hill. You come back into the Rue de Vaugirard and go some hundred yards westward till it becomes one of those typical Paris highways, narrow-based, deep as a canyon between its tall houses, long and straight as a ruled line, and leading, apparently, right out of this world. On an evening in autumn I have seen it leading, apparently, right into the setting sun. You are approaching—there it is, on the north side—a blackening boundary wall with an arched gateway in its centre, surmounted by a pediment that seems to frown down upon the pavement. It could be the ponderous and forbidding gateway leading into the forecourt of a prison; actually it leads into the forecourt of the old convent of the Carmes. There it is, and it guards—so few knowing this as they hurry about their business along the Rue de Vaugirard—what is perhaps the most terrible and the most sacred story of the Revolution. Certainly there is none more terrible and none more splendid. Looking through the gateway, you see the church of the old convent with its dome and belfry. That church and the quiet garden behind it saw for a few hours the worst things of which our broken and sundered human nature is capable, and the best.

It is Sunday, September 2nd, 1792. The Prussians and Austrians are approaching Paris to put down the Revolution; in Vendée, that maritime department of France on the Bay of Biscay, the peasants have risen against the Revolution; and the Legislative Assembly in Paris, in some panic, in a fury of resolve to save its Revolution, has called for a Terror. Danton has cried, "We cannot remain exposed both to the fire of the enemy and to that of the royalists in our midst. We must put terror into the royalists; yes, terror. *Toujours l'audace!*"

All the prisons of Paris are crowded with royalists, suspected royalists, aristocrats, and dissident priests, so their old church and convent of the Carmelites is being used as a prison for the priests of its local district, the Luxembourg district, and some others who have refused the civil oath to be loyal to the Revolution rather than to the Catholic Church. The pope has condemned the oath, defining it as "likely to annihilate completely the Christian religion"; and they have been obedient to the Holy Father's word.

Let us pass into this dark little church and stand there. It is probably empty at this busy hour of the morning, so with a little effort, undisturbed, we can see it as it was on Sunday, September 2nd, 1792.

No less than a hundred and sixty of these non-juring priests, three bishops among them, have been heaped into it, and are being held captive here. For some nights past they have slept, or tried to sleep, lying shoulder to shoulder, foot to head, on these same marble flags under your feet. Sleeping or waking, lying or standing, their eyes have seen often, because all the light falls that way, that same fresco in the dome of Elijah dropping his mantle on Elisha as he departs into heaven. They have looked at that same pulpit which is there now; at those same pictures of St. Louis of France in the chapel of the Sacred Heart; and perhaps most of all at that lovely marble statue of Virgin and Child in the north transept. At first they had hoped that their punishment might be no more than deportation; but now on this Sunday rumours have come to them that crowds are screaming around the prisons and demanding that all the "traitors" within should be sent out for death at their hands; it is said that a black flag has been broken over the Hôtel de Ville, and a tocsin rung. They have seen their usual guards replaced by these sansculottes armed with pikes and sabres and wearing the *bonnet rouge*. They have heard the gun fired from the Pont Neuf to summon the *légions libératrices,* and few now have any doubt but that they will die today. They make their confessions to one another and absolve one another.

At half-past three in the afternoon they are ordered to proceed out of the church and into the garden. " Each man looked into his heart," wrote the Abbé Frontault, one of the few who escaped, " recalled his faith, and asked God for His grace "; and so walked into the garden.

Since half past two a band of executioners commanded by the young Stanislas Maillard, who had played a foremost part in the storming of the Bastille and had led the march of the women to Versailles, have been massacring the prisoners at L'Abbaye, the prison of St. Germain des Prés, with the help of the mob in the streets around. This task completed, Maillard cries to them, " *Il n'y a plus rien à faire ici. Allons aux Carmes.*"

It is not far from St. Germain des Prés to the Carmes. The blood-splashed band, armed with pikes, sabres, pistols and hatchets, have only to rush up what is now the Rue Bonaparte, and they are in the Rue de Vaugirard. They rush along it and through the emptied church, yelling their blasphemies, and so into the garden.

But we must pass into the garden to hear the rest of the grand and terrible story. Our guide will lead us along a cloister into a passage; and along that passage to a back door; and through the back door on to a little threshold from which, on either side, four worn steps wind down on to the garden path. Note very well that dusky passage; that narrow doorway—look back upon it; and this little *perron* or stairway, with the worn stone steps on either side winding down into the garden.

It is such a quiet little garden. Do we bring the ghosts with us, or are they really there? It is laid out in square grass plots with paths running between small ash trees, chestnuts, and limes. In the centre is a round stone basin with four long stone benches and a sundial placed around it. A typical convent garden.

When the hundred and sixty priests came into the garden one of them, the Abbé Guérin (or the name may be Girault), sat on the stone bench to the left of the sundial and opened his breviary. Most of the other priests wandered along the alleys under the trees. But now out of that back door and down those winding steps came Maillard's men, brandishing their sabres and axes and pistols with bared and blood-splashed arms. Some of the priests rushed towards that wall at the back of the garden, and a few, a very few, escaped by means of the espaliers on the wall into the garden of the Bénédictines du Saint Sacrament which lay behind. The Abbé Guerin arose from his bench to meet the assassins, closing his breviary. He was instantly cut down by a sabre and then thrust through by a pike, where he lay on the ground. The little sundial stands there as a memorial to him, the first who fell. The first—but in a matter of minutes forty more priests, some of whom had fallen to their knees to receive the blows in prayer, were lying dead, or left to die, in all parts of this garden.

Now a section of the frantic assassins was running down the alleys yelling, " Where is the Archbishop of Arles? " Mgr. Jean-Marie du Lau, the Archbishop, a small, plump double-chinned man, was standing near a little oratory at the back of the garden with his vicar general. The vicar general said, " I think they have come to massacre us," and the Archbishop answered, " Ah well, my dear, if this is our moment, let us submit and thank God that we have our blood to offer in His cause." He knelt for a moment and then rose and walked towards the executioners, though his priests tried to surround him and hold him back. " Let me pass," he said. " If my blood will appease them, what does it matter that I die? Surely it is my duty to spare your days at the cost of my own." He came face to face with his hunters and, unconsciously perhaps, spoke almost exactly the words of his Master in another garden. He said to them, " I am he whom you seek."

" Is it you then, you old rascal," asked one of them, " who are the Archbishop of Arles? "

" I am he, but I have done no wrong to anyone."

" Oh, well," laughed another, " now we'll do some to you," and he swung his sabre at the Archbishop's brow.

The Archbishop lifted his hand before his eyes but the sabre of another hacked the hand off. Further blows felled him to the earth, and a pike through his breast impaled him there. His martyrdom was over.

The assassins then turned to butcher other priests, but at this moment Maillard himself, who had delayed at L'Abbaye, appeared at a window above that little double stairway into the garden. There it is today, a barred window, known always as " la fenêtre de Maillard." He shouted, " Stop all that! This has got to be done properly. That's no way to do it. Bring them in. Bring them in to be judged properly."

His men obeyed, and all the priests who were still alive, presumably some hundred of them, were herded back, past the bodies of their brothers on grass or path. They were driven up the steps, along the passage, and into the church. In the church they again gave each other absolution, lest they had offended in the meantime, and together recited the prayers for the dying.

Outside in that little dusky passage through which you came Maillard put a table just at the foot of the stairs that led to his " window," and only a few paces from that door into the garden. At the table he set one Violette as the

president of a makeshift tribunal. Violette had a list of
the prisoners before him, and in couples they were brought
from the church to be tried and judged. They answered to
their names and admitted their refusal of the civil oath.
And in every case repeated it. " *A la mort*." They were
thrust through the garden door on to the stairway and saw
all around it their eager executioners with their sabres,
axes and pikes in their blood-wet hands. Two by two they
went down the steps and died on the broad garden path
about the stairway. The stairway is known now as the
Escalier des Martyrs.

Great stories are told of the words and actions of some
of them before they came through that door and down those
steps. The Abbé Jacques Gabriel Galais, a priest of the
neighbouring St. Sulpice, and the Superior of the Séminaire
des Robertins in Paris, had been acting as a kind of mess
president for his brother prisoners in the church, getting
extra food for them from an eating-house keeper outside.
And now when he must answer to his name and go to the
tribunal in the passage and to death, he remembered that
the restaurateur had not yet been paid. So he took his
portfolio and his bills with him and said to Violette,
" Monsieur, I have not been able to see our restaurateur
and settle our account with him. But I am sure I could not
leave in safer hands all that we owe him. May I then ask
you to remit to him these three hundred and twenty-five
livres ? " Having made this courteous request, he added,
" Here too are my portfolio and my watch. Perhaps you
will sell them and devote such value as they have to the
relief of the poor "; then walked to the door and the steps.

M. the Comte de Valfons de la Calmette was the only
layman among these clerical prisoners. There was no
reason for him to accept or reject the oath. He had only
to say that he was a layman and to go free, for today, at
any rate. Who will ever know what prompted his answer
when he was asked, possibly because his clothes were

different, " Who are you and what is your profession? " Had he decided that he wished to go the same way as the good fathers with whom he had shared imprisonment and from whom he had received absolution? One cannot know, but he answered only, " I am a member of the Holy Catholic and Apostolic Church." For this he was driven to the doorway, and soon lay on the path among the priests.

The Bishop of Beauvais, François Joseph de la Roche-foucauld, had been wounded in the leg during that first assault in the garden before they had all been ordered back into the church. Some of the priests had helped him to walk back and put him in the " monks' choir " behind the high altar, presumably because there he could sit in one of the stalls. But of course he could not come to the tribunal when his name was called. Angry and eager searchers came into the church crying, " The Bishop of Beauvais. Where is the Bishop of Beauvais? " They found him in the choir, and he said to them, " Here I am. I am not refusing to go and die with the others, but as you see, I cannot walk. Have the charity, I pray you, to support and help me, so that I can go where you wish me to go."

Some priests, as I have said, escaped—there are diverging reports of the exact number who perished—but it is certain that at least a hundred and fifteen died in the garden and that their blood soaked into this earth where we stand. The majority fell in the vicinity of the Escalier des Martyrs, so that in the evening there was a great pile of them there. On the base of the escalier, facing us, is a stone plaque; on it we can see two words only, cut there with a dignity worthy of those whom they commemorate. " *Hic ceciderunt.*" Here they fell.

5

The Other Hill

5

The Other Hill

THE other hill, the Mount of the Martyrs, crowned now by Sacré Coeur de Montmartre, has no such claims to have loosed history upon the world. Steep and high, and bearing proudly the domes of Sacré Coeur, it dominates the city as no other hill, so far as I know, dominates a European capital, but it has never dominated history. After the martyrdom of St. Denis and his companions—and all this is legendary matter—the one event that really unleashed some history from up here was the coming, in 1534, of Ignatius Loyola with *his* companions to the church on the site of the martyrdom and there, in its crypt, making the stern vows which created the Society of Jesus, that disciplined army of the Jesuits whose duty was to fight in the van of the Counter-Reformation. Six others took the vows with him, four of them Spaniards like himself, one a Portuguese, and one a Savoyard. Among the Spaniards was no less a saint than Francis Xavier, the Apostle of the Indies.

The sacred grove of the Parisii, the Roman temple of Mercury and Mars, the martyrdom of St. Denis, the founding of the Jesuits—it is fair, I think, to call the Butte Montmartre our city's holy hill; and surely its holiness was never more nobly maintained than when the Sisters of the Abbaye de Montmartre, old women, middle-aged women and young girls, came down the slope to the guillotine, chanting their praises of God. That singing defeats their murderers still.

Let us climb up the hill by the road which the three martyrs took, St. Denis, St. Rustique, and St. Eleuthère.

Tradition has it that they were first tortured on the island and then led up towards the Temple of Mercury and Mars to be beheaded there, and that the route of this, their Via Dolorosa, was along the Rue Montmartre as far as the church of Notre Dame de Lorette and thence up the ever-steepening " Rue des Martyrs." But since it is likely that some of us are weaker spirits than they, and have no wish to be martyred too, walking that long and steepening

road, I suggest that we take a taxi or the Métro all the way to Pigalle, an unsaintly place, and only there begin our climb up the " Martyrs' Road."

Less than three hundred yards up the Rue des Martyrs we come to the Rue Antoinette and, turning into it on our right, come quickly upon a modern and extremely ugly grey church. This is the chapel of the Auxiliatrices du Purgatoire, or the Helpers of the Holy Souls, those good nuns who will pray for us when we are in Purgatory, or conceivably do us an even greater service, since their whole purpose is, by works of zeal and charity and by unceasing prayer, to empty Purgatory of its suffering souls and fill it instead with souls snatched from Hell. The church with the convent at its side is ugly and commonplace because erected in a bad architectural hour, 1887. None the less it is a place twice holy. First because it replaces an ancient church that covered the site where the three martyrs were beheaded, their guards having lost all patience with them because they refused to show fear, and so slaughtered them here while still quite a way from the top of the hill. Here then it was that St. Denis stooped and picked up his severed head and carried it over the hill-top for a mile or two till he dropped dead and was buried by a pious woman where now stands the Basilica of St. Denis. (When the Cardinal de Polignac told to Madame du Deffand this story of St. Denis bending down to recover his head and then carrying it a couple of leagues, and said that it was only at first that St. Denis found the journey difficult, she answered, " But I can well believe it, Monsieur. It was only the first step that was really remarkable.")

For seventeen hundred years there have been pilgrimages here for those who would honour, and have their part in, the cult of St. Denis and his fellow martyrs. But this is not all. On August 15th, 1534, the Feast of the Assumption, a lean and stern Spanish soldier, disabled in the wars, Don Inigo de Loyola, came with his six friends to this ancient church and there in its crypt bound themselves to be the shock-troops of the Catholic Church, fighting for it against Heresy and Infidelity everywhere. Church and crypt have completely disappeared, the Revolution having rooted up even their foundation stones, but in 1855 a devout priest, the Abbé le Rebours, traced on old maps and plans the exact site of this crypt of St. Denis and St. Ignatius, and in time this present church was built with a crypt that resembled as far as possible that in which St. Ignatius knelt with his friends, and the Society of Jesus was born.

The Auxiliatrices du Purgatoire now have the care of it

The church of St. Germain des Prés, showing also, opposite, the Café des Deux Magots and part of the Café de Flore, both famous rendezvous of the writers and artists of Paris

Diane de Poitiers' house (right) in the Cour de Rohan

Montmartre. Le Bateau Lavoir, tenement of the artists and cradle of Cubism

Rue de l'Abreuvoir, Montmartre

The artists of Montmartre

Place du Tertre, Montmartre

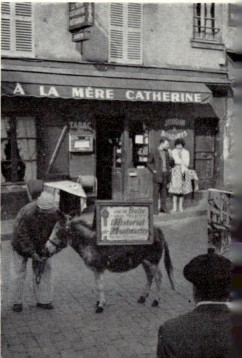

Balloon seller below Sacré Coeur

Place du Tertre,
Montmartre

and if you ring at their convent door one of them will, at
no cost to you, take you into their cloistered garden and
guide you to the crypt. She will probably leave you there,
and that is well, because it is not a little thing to stand
on the stones of this crypt and see in imagination Ignatius
Loyola kneeling there with Peter Faber, Francis Xavier,
Diego Laynez, Alfonso Salmeron, Nicolas Alfonso de
Bobadilla and Simon Rodriguez, all consecrating themselves
to a merciless discipline in the eternal warfare for God;
not a little thing to watch the Society of Jesus being born
here and wrapped in its swaddling bands, and to think of
all that the Jesuits have wrought since in the old world and
the new.

The hill is less holy now. Its saints for the last hundred
years and more have been the artists who, vowed to the
Goddess of Art, have lived their consecrated lives up here,
while they served her in poverty, chastity and obedience—
well, in poverty, anyhow. For the most part, like the
Norse gods, they have lived on or about the top of the
mountain. Here are a few of these latter-day saints who,
here on the Butte, have lived and slaved and laughed loud,
or despaired and despaired, but worked on, often drinking
deep, too deep, in the Lapin Agile or the Bonne Franquette
with their models at their sides or on their knees, and paying
their shot, when they had no money, with canvases from
their studios and their attics: Corot, Van Gogh, Gauguin,
Renoir, Toulouse-Lautrec, Picasso, Van Dongen, Vlaminck,
Modigliani, Raoul Dufy, Utrillo. It was in the garden of
the Bonne Franquette that Van Gogh painted " La Guin-
gette," which you can see (and should see) in the Jeu de
Paume in the Garden of the Tuileries, together with many
other miracles wrought by these martyrs in the latter half of
the last century. To this name, Musée du Jeu de Paume,
were this book a Baedeker, I would attach, not two aster-
isks or three, but almost all I could find, because within

the museum's small area you can see so exquisitely hung and shown, almost all the famous pictures of the Impressionists, to whose work it is now devoted.

If you would see what kind of hives they often lived in, turn into the Rue Cortot, just off the summit, and consider that at No. 12 there have lived Renoir, Bernard, Suzanne Valadon, her son Utrillo, Raoul Dufy and many others. Or, better still, come a little way down from the summit to the Place Emile Goudeau and take a look at that poor cracked stucco tenement building, long and low and ramshackle, No. 13. Here lived Picasso, Modigliani, Max Jacob, André Salmon, and others who have never won such fame as these, but have dreamed of it, all the same. They are still there, the artists, labouring in the service of beauty and in the hope of fame. Peep in at the long wooden passages and you will see their cards on the cracking doors of their studios. The place is known as the " Bateau Lavoir," or " Laundry Boat," because some of the artists have thought it looked like one of the boats from which washerwomen launder linen in the Seine. I cannot help thinking that they have observed this resemblance only at night sometimes, after hearty drinking at the Lapin Agile and a visit or two to other well-loved bistrots on the Butte. The Bateau Lavoir is a very famous name, for here, in this poor hutment, Cubism was born—born with Picasso for its father and Max Jacob for its sponsor and prophet. " I paint objects as I think them, not as I see them," said Picasso, and, coming out of that door before you, brought Cubism into the world. Conceptual art, rather than perceptual, was henceforth the aim and only desire of all up-to-date young men, and the movement towards wholly abstract painting and sculpture had begun.

So while this hill may not have released the current of the Revolution which shook all the kingdoms of the world, it did send down from this dilapidated tenement a stream which shook all the smaller kingdoms of Art.

They tell many tales on the Butte of Cubism and its origins here; of the Groupe du Bateau Lavoir which was formed in 1908 and included, besides Picasso and Max Jacob, Braque and Apollinaire and Juan Gris and André Simon and Gertrude Stein. One such story is that of Picasso who, after making a fine study of packing cases as they were being unloaded on the quays, called it " Portrait of My Father."

But for me the artist who haunts the Butte is none of these; it is Maurice Utrillo who paid little attention to the Cubists, his contemporaries, and went his own way. If you would see what he loved to paint, you have only to climb a few steps from the Bateau Lavoir to the narrow mouth of the Rue Saint Rustique. Here is old Montmartre indeed. Look up its narrow vista to that glimpse at its end of Sacré Coeur's white dome, and you are looking at one of Utrillo's most famous pictures. If you can see his dream-light on the old plastered and shuttered houses, his blues and pinks on the cobbles, his golden browns on the lurched and leprous walls, and the tragic vision that lights it all, then you have eyes worthy of him and are the one for whom he stood here and painted it.

If you would picture him here, standing behind his easel, he is probably in ragged clothes, his trousers tied with string about his waist, his feet in worn slippers. The face that lifts regularly from canvas to street, and to that distant glimpse of Sacré Coeur, is yellow and sunken, with dark melancholy eyes and dark drooping moustache. Maybe he staggers a little when he steps back a few paces to see his picture as a whole; for more often than not, when Maurice Utrillo is seen on Montmartre, he is in a drunken or half-drunken state.

There are innumerable little picture-shops all over the Butte, and there is one at the corner of the Rue Saint Rustique. I went into it one day and asked the proprietor if he had a picture of Utrillo's, meaning of course a copy. But he thought, or pretended to think, that I meant an original, and said, laughing, " Find me a million dollars and I will get you one."

This was within a few feet of the spot where Utrillo stood, hungry and in rags, painting.

It is good to think that Utrillo was one of those painters, not too many, who knew their fame and enjoyed prosperity before they died.

The Place du Tertre is, as its name implies, on the top of the hill; it is the centre of old Montmartre, but it hides a little coyly, I always fancy, from the white purity of Sacré Coeur. It was the old village square in the days of the windmills, the vineyards, and the godly nuns; and today with its old trees and small low houses it has something of the look of a village green. Always the artists in their berets are standing at its corners with their easels, painting the pleasant scene, and the American visitors are standing everywhere with their expensive cameras photographing the artists. In this Place du Tertre it is possible to imagine that you are hearing only American voices and the English tongue. Possible also to imagine that one of those artists will one day be in the crowned company that includes Renoir, Lautrec, Van Gogh and Utrillo. Some of them, for a price, will paint *you* instead of Sacré Coeur.

At night when all the light in the Place du Tertre is held under the awnings of the cafés and falls yellow on the tables and the cobbles, beneath a night-blue, star-spattered sky, you are instantly reminded of Van Gogh's "Café at Night," even though he painted this in Arles, under a southern sky.

But whether you sit at those tables at night, or under the brightly coloured sunshades in the daytime, you will pay such prices as are made to match the highest point in Paris; and on the whole it is best to leave the tables under awnings or sunshades and to go and sit on the terrace under Sacré Coeur, for here you will see the whole Paris basin of which we spoke in our first chapter lying beneath your eyes. It is green and wooded and empty no more, but crowded from hill to hill with roofs, towers, chimneys, terraces, domes, spires—all the *toits de Paris*, and all slightly bathed in the mist of a northern valley. The vast conspectus is closed for you by the dome of the Panthéon on St. Geneviève's hill, across the Seine.

I have little heart to leave the top of the Butte and the kingdom of the artists for the lower slopes and the kingdom of the *établissements de nuit*. If you want them, they are in and about the Place Pigalle and the Place Blanche. Here are the Moulin Rouge and the Chat Noir and the Eve de Paris and the Galas de Striptease Internationaux, all the places mischievously advertised as " *interdits aux gens sérieux*," where you can see the " *reines du deshabillage froufroutant*." Here is the night life of Montmartre but to what degree the customers of this nocturnal trade, the students of the marching young ladies dressed only in three sequinned patches—or possibly only one—are far more British and American than Parisian I have no means of measuring.

Before we descend to these places, and it seems fitting they should function on the lower slopes, we must I suppose go and look at the Lapin Agile, because in the early days of this century it was the rendezvous of so many writers, painters and poets on Montmartre. It is a little way down the Rue des Saules which runs northward from the mouth

of our Rue Saint Rustique: a little rustic tavern behind a tree; standing just below the walled vineyard which is kept here to bear witness to the days when Montmartre was a hill with windmills on its crown, and vineyards all down its sunny slopes.

Alas, a decline is already patent here, for the Lapin Agile is now a theatrical little place more suited to a stage scene than an honest street; its rustic fence, apparently made of tree branches, is really made of concrete, and one feels inclined to examine bole and branches of the old twisted tree and see if they are made of painted concrete too.

That concrete paling twists the heart. And yet . . . let us get behind the concrete, behind the vulgar tricks of today, and try to see the Lapin as it was on some autumn night during the decade before the First War when the rustic paling wasn't there at all, and the old tree was young, and no self-conscious creeper draped its tresses archly over the tavern door. Over the tavern door instead is only the legend "*Cce. de Vins Traiteur.*" This is an honest little wayside inn with its painted sign showing an agile rabbit leaping into a saucepan with a bottle in its paw. This was painted by A. Gill, and I suppose the name of the inn is in part a pun. Tonight there are sounds of singing and laughter within, so we will enter to share the fun. We come to a long room beneath a low dark ceiling. It is furnished with a long table and benches, and the smoky light in the room is ruddy because the lamps are shaded with red silk handkerchiefs. Pinned to the walls are odd sketches or paintings by Utrillo, Picasso and others, some of which, no doubt, have been given to the landlord as payment for a night of gaiety and wine. Frédéric, the landlord, who loves his artist customers, Frédé, as they all call him, is seated at the table with his guitar, and since it is a wild night on the hill and most of the usual frequenters have felt the call of Frédé's wine, he has a big crowd with him, seated or standing round the table. Most are in their twenties, and all are very poor. Among them are Roland Dorgelès, Pierre MacOrlan, Max Jacob, Pablo Picasso, Guillaume Apollinaire, Francis Carco, Suzanne Valadon and Maurice Utrillo, her son. Or it could be (for too often it is so) that Utrillo is lying drunk on one of the benches. Some of the boys' mistresses are with them, no gold-diggers these, because there is no gold to dig, but good, understanding girls who when asked what they will drink answer, " The cheapest there is."

Now one of the company rises to sing his song, and then another to recite verses of his own. Song and poem, for all we know, are the only payment they can offer to Frédé tonight. But as such he will accept their performances—for tonight, and perhaps tomorrow night, and until their days are better, with a picture sold, a poem printed. How Frédéric kept the Lapin afloat and profitable for so long, I do not know, with patrons such as these.

But they have repaid him, some of them. Did not Utrillo more than once paint a picture, now famous, of the front of the Lapin Agile; and is not the sad pale woman in Picasso's haunting picture, " The Woman with the Jack-daw," old Frédé's daughter?

All of them are dispersed now, many to death, and nearly all to some degree of fame as painters and poets and novelists. In a sad little poem Francis Carco has sung his nostalgia for days at the Lapin and friends he loved there, fifty years ago.

Tout le jour je vous ai cherchés
Comme au temps de notre jeunesse,
Dans les cafés . . . Ce temps renaisse
Et nos amours et nos pêches . . .
Je vous ai cherchés en moi-même
Comme un disparu, ceux qu'il aime
Les appelle, et se tient caché . . .

With those gentle words in our minds let us go on down the hill. Going down, we pass the Moulin de la Galette and look at it sadly, a crude and carpentered dance hall dolled up for English and American visitors, but once loved and painted and sung; by Renoir, Corot, Lautrec, Van Gogh, Utrillo—by Renoir in perhaps his most celebrated picture of all, *Le Moulin de la Galette,* one more world-famous canvas that can be seen in the Jeu de Paume, blazing its dominant blues from a dove-grey wall. Do not miss it. I will repeat the address: Musée du Jeu de Paume, Garden of the Tuileries, at the very corner of the Rue de Rivoli and the Place de la Concorde.

We come down from the hill by the Rue Lepic which turns and tacks and twists because it was made in the Second Empire as an easier ascent for the horses and horsed carriages of that lively time. By the Rue Blanche which succeeds it we come again upon the broad bottom of the basin or valley; upon, that is to say, the Plain and Marsh of Paris.

6

The Streets on Plain and Marsh

6

The Streets on Plain and Marsh

EMBRACED by the shoulders of Montmartre, which end left and right, at Père Lachaise and at the Arc de Triomphe, lies the plain and marsh of Paris. Across the river, embraced by the left shoulder of Mont Sainte Geneviève lies the city's other plain, the Plain of Issy, but at present we are speaking only of this crescent-shape segment north of the river and beneath the shoulders of the northern hill. All this is famous ground. It is the site of the old Gothic city and of François Premier's Paris and Henry of Navarre's.

The Gothic city was one of high-pointed gables, steep spires, and sturdy ornamented towers, all of it girded by the stout old towered wall of King Philip Augustus. In its deep and narrow thoroughfares, many of which are still there though changed, you must imagine, not the Legions marching, but the mailed knights riding sometimes, on their short but powerful horses. The ancient Roman road still pierced the Gothic city, straight as a Roman spear, from the Pont Notre Dame to the Porte St. Martin. The medieval streets wound tortuously—and usually stinkingly—through the swarm of gabled houses, and the present Rue Chanoinesse in the precincts of Notre Dame follows the course of one of them, where Héloïse lived and loved.

Very little survives of the Gothic city; very little, that is, in stone and mortar; but much, very much, in the things that are invisible: the law learnt from Rome; the soul of the university; the new French tongue and the vernacular literature; and the sense of France as a nation and of Paris as its capital. The few stone monuments that remain of the twelfth century, how buoyant and proud and eager they are: Notre Dame, Sainte Chapelle. Of the fourteenth and fifteenth centuries again we have all too few heirlooms: the lovely Hôtel de Cluny; the flamboyant ambulatory of St. Séverin's church which is nothing less than a grove of palms in stone; and lastly—lastly in its exact sense—the Tour St. Jacques-la-Boucherie.

The Tour St. Jacques, which still towers there and looks at Notre Dame without shame, was the last flourish of the High Gothic in the face of the new Classical, or Renaissance, style which was to sweep it out of Europe for ever—but what a flourish! The sixteenth century came with its new learning and its new architecture; and, heedless of it or gaily defying it, the Tour St. Jacques went up, not completed till 1522, so that the students of the new learning on the hill across the river, Calvin, Loyola, Rabelais, those sons of a new world, must have watched it rising within its high scaffolding, joyously, defiantly. The joy still shows in its stones; the defiance, I sometimes think, laughs from its gargoyles. Perhaps there is a symbol of the way it bridges one of History's most salient changes in culture, taste and thought in the fact that the old Gothic church of St. Jacques-la-Boucherie which once belonged to it has disappeared and it now stands alone as a towering canopy over the statue of Blaise Pascal—Pascal who used it for his barometric experiments rather as Galileo used the Leaning Tower of Pisa to demonstrate the laws of falling bodies; Pascal the mathematician, physicist, inventor, and yet austerely religious man; Pascal who seems to bridge so perfectly the ages of religion and of reason.

The Renaissance City may be said to begin with Francis I who came to the throne in 1515 when the Tour St. Jacques was still rising. Its most famous monument today is, of course, the Louvre. I shall not take you inside the Louvre,

I dare not, because to guide anyone properly through its galleries would require twenty such books as this (and they can all be bought at the entrance), but we will look at the outside of it here and there. It was Philip Augustus who, in 1200, placed a square and moated fortress (later called the Louvre, no one really knows why) on the bank of the Seine down river, precisely as William the Conqueror placed the square and moated Tower of London on the Thames bank down river, as a bastion to watch over and threaten the dangerous approach from the sea. The Louvre guarded the western approach; later the huge square, eight-towered and moated Bastille rose across the city's eastern gate, the Porte St. Antoine. But by this time, three hundred years later, the tactical importance of Philip Augustus's fortress down river was lost because it was now far inside the new bastioned wall of Charles V; it was now nothing but an uncomfortable palace for the kings.

So Francis I decided to have much of it down and to build a new and fine palace there for himself and his successors. If you will walk through the long colonnaded front of the Louvre into its Cour Carrée, the enclosed square or courtyard, you will see in its south-west corner the outline of the fortress's straight walls and round towers traced in the paving with lines of asphalt and stones; and you will realise at once how like it was to our Tower of London.

But now, standing exactly where you are in the Cour Carrée, look up from the ground; look up at the south-western façade of the existing Louvre; that is to say, the façade on the left of the clock in its tower. It is the oldest part of the palace which Francis wanted but did not live to see; it was built and completed in the reign of his son, Henry II. You are looking at the work of one of the world's greatest architects, Pierre Lescot, and at the sculptures of one of the world's greatest sculptors, Jean Goujon. Note only those reliefs that decorate both the frames of the top-floor windows and the segmental pediments above them. How exquisitely those nudes, kneeling, crouching, seated, dreaming, playing, harmonise with, sustain, and unassumingly embellish the lines and lintels of the windows. One and all they are fit for the company of the painted but architectural figures in Michelangelo's Sistine roof. There is no other façade of the many that make up the present Louvre to equal in interest this one of Pierre Lescot and Jean Goujon; not only because of its early Renaissance date but because of its beauties, which are outside Time.

Into Paris now, and into History, and most energetically into the French Renaissance, comes—with gaiety, laughter and a magnanimity quite uncharacteristic of these years (and indeed and alas of most years)—King Henry of Navarre, now Henry IV of France, *le bon roi Henri*. " The King has come to marshal us In all his armour dressed," sang Macaulay of Henry of Navarre at the Battle of Ivry, and it seems an apt line to greet him now.

But we must set the stage for this most attractive figure; and we are well placed to do so, standing in the Cour Carrée. Only walk back through the central archway into the Place du Louvre and look at the church of St. Germain l'Auxerrois immediately opposite you. But you must imagine it, not in the light of day, but in the blue, if luminous, darkness of a Paris midnight. Midnight passes and it is now the dark early morning of August 24th, 1572. Great numbers of Huguenots, as the Protestants are called, are still in Paris after the marriage, on a platform before Notre Dame, of the Queen Mother's daughter, Marguerite de Valois, a girl of nineteen, to a young man of the same age, who is Henry, the new Protestant king of Navarre. But the Queen Mother, Catherine de' Medici and many other Catholics, not least among the priests, the Jesuits and the kindred religious orders, are still astounded, horrified, even maddened, by this marriage. Their anger, their hate, their furious jealousy for the Faith as they see it, are brooding monstrously under the night sky behind the hush in the city; for Paris is quiet, as quiet as it can ever be, at this hour, between half past one and two in this morning of August 24th, 1572. But those who know, wait. Then, suddenly, the belfry of St. Germain l'Auxerrois (not the flamboyant octagonal tower directly in front of you, which is a modern erection, but the old square belfry rising behind the south transept) shakes as its great bell rings out, strangely and alarmingly, a call. Instantly all the steeples of the city repeat on their bells this master call; and, answering it, assassins rush from hiding places in every quarter of Paris with white crosses in their hats to identify them, and lists of condemned victims in their hands. They rush first to the houses of the Huguenots, which have been secretly marked, and, forcing their way in, murder in their beds, or out of them, all whom they can find, men, women, servants, children. Thence into the streets, crying, " *Vive la messe! Mort aux Huguenots! Vive le roi!* " to find other victims and to pursue a massacre that will last throughout the rest of that night and all the next day, till dusk comes down and it is dark again. Catherine, the Queen Regent, who had forced her young son, Charles IX, to assent to this remedy for the ills of Protestantism, watched the slaughter from a window of the Louvre, and it is said that Charles, from another window, fired with his arquebus at the Protestants running for their lives along the quay below; good sport; and that at the end of the day he asked of Catherine de' Medici, " How have I played my little part, Mother? "

Along all the quays and banks of the Seine Queen Mother and King must have seen the murderers throwing dead bodies, mostly stripped naked, into the river—that Seine beside you which, like our Thames, is so assuredly " liquid history."

August 24th is the Feast of St. Bartholomew and gives its name to the massacre. But though begun in the small hours of that morning the running slaughter was resumed or continued in Paris and in the great cities of France for days afterwards. Some have estimated that ten thousand were killed in Paris and thirty thousand throughout the kingdom.

News of the massacre was received in Rome as a cause for jubilation so great that Pope and cardinals went in state to give thanks to God for it. The Pope, Gregory XIII, struck a medal to commemorate the glorious day. The reverse of this medal shows an angel with uplifted cross and bared sword slaughtering Huguenots, of whom one is a woman. Above angel and victims runs the inscription, " Ugonottorum · Strages · 1572." " Slaughter of the Huguenots, 1572." In this year of the Bartholomew the wise, tolerant, melancholy, witty, shoulder-shrugging Montaigne retired to his château in Périgord to give the rest of his days to meditation, study, and the writing of essays; to consecrate, as a Latin inscription on the walls of his cabinet states, " this his ancestral seat and pleasant retiring place to liberty, tranquillity and leisure." In one of the essays he declared his adhesion for ever to " the Apostolic and Roman Catholic Church in which I was born and in which I shall die," but he wrote in another, sadly, " Our religion is made to extirpate our vices; instead it covers them, nourishes them, incites them."

All such attempts at suppression by violence and terror (and will the advocates of violence and strong-arm methods ever perceive this?) achieve in the end the opposite of their aims. History shows that this never fails to be the ultimate issue. Enough, then, to say that surviving Huguenots formed themselves into rebel organisations, chose after a time as their obvious leader (and never was a better choice) the young prince, King Henry of Navarre, declared him heir to the throne—was he not descended from St. Louis?— and after twelve years of the " wars of religion," in which they would go into battle crying, " Remember St. Bartholomew! " and after a siege of Paris during which the people were reduced to eating grass and disinterred corpses, saw him enter Paris as its King. True that he had consented to become a Catholic, since that was the religion of most of his subjects, but he had won for the Protestants the assurance of their religious liberty, their political enfranchisement and their civil rights, all of which he later proclaimed in the Edict of Nantes.

After St. Louis, who was a king out of Time since he was greater than any single age, Henry of Navarre, despite his faults, which were certainly unsaintly but never completely unamiable, was the most attractive of all French kings. Louis XIV, *le Roi Soleil,* what love had he to compare with that which Henry IV, *le bon roi Henri,* sometimes called Henri le Grand, won in his life and has maintained in the memory of Frenchmen for three and a half centuries? " His mischievously sparkling eyes," André Maurois has written, " his arched nose, his square beard, his Gascon accent, his delightful character, and even his love affairs, soon became popular."

Ah yes, those love affairs—we must come to them in due course.

Once he had been pronounced King of France by his predecessor, Henry III, on his deathbed, his desire was to love, guide and protect all his people, even though most of them were still fighting to keep him off the throne and out of Paris, the capital. One day he rode to the top of Montmartre and, looking down upon the city that would not take him in, dreamed great things for it when he should be its master. Then there should be forgiveness for all his foes, a general amnesty, so that he could be king of a united people and not of a faction only. " Those who honestly follow their conscience," he said, " are of my religion, and, as for me, I belong to the faith of all who are gallant and good." And again: " We are all Frenchmen and fellow-citizens of the same fatherland; therefore we must be brought to agreement by reason and kindness and not by strictness and cruelty, which serve only to arouse men."

His wit, his gift of phrase, and his good Gascon blunt-ness shine out in many of his famous utterances. Besieging Paris, he let the food go through, saying, " I do not wish to rule over a cemetery." After his victory at Arques he wrote to his friend, Crillon, " Go, hang yourself, brave Crillon; we fought at Arques, and you were not there; but I love you just the same." At Ivry before the battle began he tied a white plume to his helmet—" The King has come to marshal us In all his armour dressed And he has bound a snow-white plume Upon his gallant crest "— and he shouted to his captains and his men, " My friends, yonder is the enemy; here is your king. If you should lose your standards, rally round my white plume; you will always find it in the path of victory and honour." His best-known words, " Paris is well worth a mass," sound cynical enough, and no doubt his motives for accepting Catholicism were less than pure, but in part the words covered with a jest his desire to do the only thing that could end the wars and unite the kingdom. " Instruct me, my lords," he said to the bishops, " I am not stubborn. Maybe I can jump the ditch." And, accord-ing to Maurois, he then led my lords a rare dance with his questions and comments, even going to the length of asking whether the cult of the saints was not "a kind of leg-pulling." Directly he had captured Paris he made peace with Spain and went and sat in a window of the Porte St. Denis to watch the Spanish soldiers, whom Philip had sent to help the Catholics fight him, march in good order

out of his capital. " My greetings to your master," he
shouted to them from his window, " but don't come
back! " With the Duke of Sully, his ever loyal but often
cantankerous follower and later his great but grumbling
minister, who, though accepting as inevitable the King's
conversion, kept pictures of Calvin and Luther in his
room to tease him, Henry would laugh and say, " Go on;
the hour when you no longer ridicule me or contradict me,
I shall believe you no longer love me." He paid all the
debts of his most ferocious enemy, the Duke of Mayenne
who had led the armies against him, but allowed himself a
ration of vengeance by " making the big rheumatic fellow
keep up with his quick strides for a time."

But those love affairs. The people were amused by them
and perhaps the better able to countenance them in their
relief at these evidences of virility after the odd behaviour
of his predecessor, Henry III, who called his young male

favourites his " little darlings " and liked them to be
gaily bedecked, while he himself wore necklaces and
bracelets and walked prettily in an expanding aura of scent.
Such a dainty and prancing king offered the country little
hope of an heir, but no such doubt could be held of Henry
of Navarre. Certainly his first wife, Marguerite de Valois,
had given him no children, but this, says Maurois with
French wit, " was most certainly not because of his impot-
ence since he produced a flourishing crop of bastards. His
amorous escapades were beyond number: history has dug
up the names of more than fifty-six of his mistresses—and
Clio does not know all." If the allusion were permissible
in such a grave book as this, one might speak of fifty-seven
varieties. His virility, after he had put away Marguerite
de Valois, was adequately established by his new queen's
annual pregnancies.

The king was hardly in Paris before the noise of the
stonemasons was heard everywhere. The creation of his
dream of Paris as a city of Renaissance order, grace and
beauty had begun. If you would see the dream of Henry
standing intact before you, and the domestic architecture
of the Renaissance standing there almost in perfection
though three hundred and fifty years have passed, you must
come to the Place des Vosges in the Bastille district of
Paris, which is the old marsh area, the Quartier du Marais.
It is in the east end of the city, well off the tourist track;
it is forlorn and decayed; its stone is crumbled and its
plaster cracked; the children of the poor run and scream
in it; it is lost, so to say, in the city's industrial quarter and
behind the squalid streets of St. Antoine; but there it is; the
huge square with its gracefully proportioned houses or
" pavilions," all red brick and white stone beneath the
blue-grey slates of their high mansard roofs; and as you
come out of some narrow street into this ample and open
place, you seem to have stepped out of our present cramped,
hurrying, profit-driven age and to be standing, not only

in a past long dead, but in a peaceful moment of the past when for a little, under the impact of a good king, the time was leisured and lively and gracious.

There it is, before your eyes, with the children of the workers at their shrill games in its park-like central garden, and the old men with their pipes dreaming on the seats there, and the tired working-women resting on them with their loads. Known for two centuries as the Place Royale, it was specially built to the order of Henry who intended that the central pavilion on the south side should be his own, " The King's Pavilion," and the opposite one on the north side the Queen's. From the medallion high up on his pavilion his face, bearded and smiling a little, looks down upon his now neglected and dilapidated creation.

The great square was not completed till two years after his death but throughout his century it was the most fashionable quarter of Paris. The high-railed garden in its centre, large as a park, was the promenade for all that was courtly and much that was *précieuse* in the society of the time, and it soon became the duelling ground *de rigueur* for gentlemen of culture. Henry had desired that the garden should be spacious enough for equestrian sports and parades, and it was, in fact, inaugurated before an enormous throng of courtly spectators with an " equestrian ballet " and a tournament, accompanied by an orchestra of a hundred and fifty musicians and the guns of the Bastille nearby. What do those noisy children today, and those quiet old men with their pipe-dreams, and the tired working-women on the seats know of this? May we read anything —the humour of acceptance perhaps—in the smile on the King's face as he looks down from his medallion upon the present scene?

Look round upon the thirty-six " pavilions " that frame the railed garden, with their faded brick, fallen plaster, and crumbled white stone, and their steep mansard roofs rising into the clean, blue Paris sky. In some of them lived people most famous in their century. Madame de Sévigné was born at No. 1, just by the King's Pavilion. At No. 21 lived Cardinal Richelieu. At No. 11 lived the great courtesan, Marion de l'Orme, and it is whispered that the Cardinal was among the many who enjoyed the favours of this lovely neighbour. At another house—I do not know which, but at an opposite extreme, we may say, among the mansions of morality—dwelt Monsieur Vincent, whose later name as St. Vincent de Paul is among those which do something to sweeten the vicious, cruel and bloodthirsty history of our humankind. Other famous names among the residents of the Place Royale in its fashionable days are Corneille—one of his earliest dramas is called " La Place Royale "—Condé, Bossuet, Molière, and Turenne, Marshal General of France. In addition to these historic persons you may, if you are of a fanciful turn, see many shades from French fiction walking in the garden. Who are those four men meeting under a tree and laughing so boisterously together—are they not Athos, Porthos, Aramis and D'Artagnan?

The glory departed from the Place Royale when Louis XIV towards the end of that century, in 1682, deserted Paris for the vast splendours of Versailles. The square even lost its name and was given the name of the Place des Vosges because that department of France was the first to pay a large tax in the time of the Revolution. Nevertheless some famous names of the nineteenth century belong to this nobly born, if now distressed and decaying square. Rachel Félix, whom we know as Rachel, the tragedienne, lived at No. 9, Alphonse Daudet at some other house, and Victor Hugo at No. 6, which is now the Victor Hugo Museum. Was he drawn here to be within sight of No. 11 where Marion de l'Orme had lived, about whom he wrote an excellent and untrue play?

Far the most imposing monument to King Henry of France and Navarre, and to his love of his city, is the

Grande Galerie of the Louvre, stretching for more than a quarter of a mile along the Seine's northern bank and therefore called also the Galerie du Bord de l'Eau. His desire was to continue the Palace of the Louvre in the beautiful fashion of Lescot and Goujon that we saw in the Cour Carrée. The Grande Galerie is not the equal of that façade but it displays all the exuberant life and joyous art of the Renaissance. It was really Henry who began to use the Seine as a beautiful and deciding factor in the building of a great city—a use of its river that London has never achieved. I can only ask you to walk that quarter-mile along the Quai du Louvre and the Quai des Tuileries and, looking up at the Grande Galerie which will flank you all the way, consider the Tuscan pilasters, the severely rectangular first story, and then the joyous second story with its statues in the niches and its high windows with their fluted pilasters and lively ornament, all leading up to the alternately triangular and rounded pediments which crown the long façade.

It being Henry's façade there was mischief in it, for he interlaced with his own initials on the stones those of his best-loved mistress, Gabrielle d'Estrées. He had wanted to marry Gabrielle and make her his queen, but Marguerite de Valois, though willing to have her marriage to him annulled, was not, as we say nowadays, " falling for this," and he married Marie de' Medici instead, and Marie was not slow to have those initials effaced; for which, I think, we can forgive her.

Come back now along the Quai du Louvre and turn with a legitimate thrill on to the Pont Neuf. This, the oldest surviving bridge in Paris despite its name, is always spoken of as Henry IV's bridge, and rightly, though it was begun before he came to the throne, its first stone being laid by his epicene predecessor, Henry III, who came to the ceremony with his eyes red with weeping for one of his little darlings. But it was Henry IV who enthusiastically

gave himself to its completion and was the first person to
ride across it. London has never fallen in love with any
one of its bridges—and, to be sure, it would be difficult to
feel a stab at the heart when thinking of Blackfriars or
Westminster bridges—but Paris has always loved her Pont
Neuf. It has been as much written about, sung about,
painted, and made the scene of opera or romance, as has
the Quartier Latin or the Parvis Notre Dame or the moulins
and streets of Montmartre. Perhaps because it had the
first pavements ever seen in Paris—an engaging curiosity;
perhaps because of its breadth and the charming round
bays that surmount its piers, it became the setting for a
permanent fair, with flower girls, mountebanks, tumblers,
hawkers and cheap-jacks, all entertaining or cheating (or
both) the gaily eddying crowds. It was the place for the
bookstalls which have ever since hugged the Seine. It was
the processional way for the entry of each new king after
each new revolution. It heard Danton's great voice in-
citing the people to revolution, and it saw his tumbril go
by, bringing him from the Conciergerie to the guillotine.

It is accepted as Henry IV's bridge, and therefore his
equestrian statue stands on the little Place du Pont Neuf
attached to its midst, backed by the trees of the Square du
Vert Galant (the square is a perfect triangle, but what
matter?). It is a fine statue, and I never come over the bridge
late at night and see it standing alone on its stage above the
river without wishing to adapt Lionel Johnson's lines about
the equestrian statue of Charles I at Charing Cross.

> Lonely and calm he rides,
> Hard by his own Whitehall.
> Only the night-wind glides;
> No crowds or rebels brawl . . .

The witty Parisians like to say that the equestrian statues
of their kings stand among the people they loved most:
Louis XIV in the Place des Victoires among the tax

collectors; Louis XIII in the old Place Royale where his favourites swarmed; and Henry of Navarre, their well-loved Henry IV, in the very centre of his city and the heart of his people.

For a tail-piece to these descriptions of the public works of Henry IV, I will subjoin here a little allusion to one of his more private messuages, for the sake of those who like to see something in Paris that only a few know of, and that is of a private nature and scandalous withal.

Come away from the Pont Neuf to the Left Bank and walk along the Quai des Grands Augustins till you come to a brief and decrepit side-street called the Rue Gît-le-Coeur. Turn into it and look up at No. 12. Even go into the broad dark entry of No. 12 and look at those steep, narrow stairs in the deep dusk of a far corner. Those steps knew the feet of Henry of Navarre, for this house, now dirty, dingy, and cankered, was one of the homes of Gabrielle d'Estrées, the King's best love. Gabrielle must have heard his feet on those stairs. I do not know the exact dates when she lived in this house, but it is pleasant to think that the three children whom she bore to her royal lover, raced up and down and jumped up and down, as children will, on this stairway. It is pleasant also to stand in the now smelly little water-side street and, looking up at the house's large first-floor windows, think of Gabrielle watching through them for her king and lover. Gabrielle d'Estrées died in

Southern arm of the Pont Neuf showing (left) the two Louis XIII houses which flank the entrance to the Place Dauphine

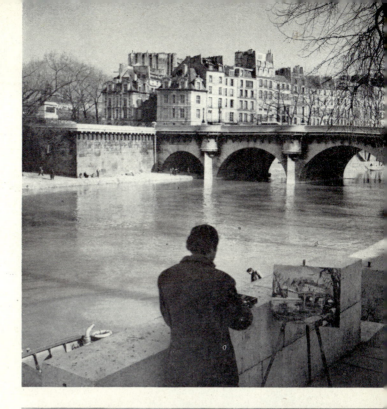

Equestrian statue of Henri Quatre on the Pont Neuf, 1614, broken and overthrown in the Revolution, restored and replaced 1818

Place des Vosges, once the Place Royale, now surrounded by the working-class areas of St. Antoine and the Bastille

The Pont Neuf
by night

prolonged and convulsive agonies, and the world was told that the cause of her death was eclampsia, a disease of pregnancy, but it may be that she was poisoned by those statesmen who wished her out of the way lest the King should marry her. Maybe she was best effaced like her initials on the Galerie du Bord de l'Eau.

Henry died quickly and with little pain. On the afternoon of May 14th, 1610, at about four o'clock, his fine royal coach was carrying him and a few gentlemen to visit his cantankerous minister and teasing friend, the Duc de Sully. In the narrow Rue de la Ferronerie the advance of the coach was impeded by haycarts and wagons and brought to a standstill. A tall young schoolmaster, François Ravaillac, who had been waiting his chance, leapt on to a stationary wheel and, seeing the King reading a letter, stabbed him with his poniard. He struck a second time, and this blow found the King's heart. " *Ce n'est rien . . .*" said the King to his companions crowding about him. " *Ce n'est rien . . .*" and died.

They took his body into the Louvre and laid it in state in a bedroom. Then a wax effigy was made of their murdered king and it lay for ten days in the Salle des Caryatides of the Louvre; later his coffin rested in this same place. Now this Salle des Caryatides you are bound to visit because it is the first great room which you come to when you visit the Old Louvre. And as you halt in it and look about you at the sculptures of Hellenistic times, at Love Overcoming the Centaur, and Aphrodite Surprised, and after you have given your admiration, perhaps a breathless admiration, to the four tall caryatides of Jean Goujon which support the tribune, then think for a moment of Henry's body lying here. Remember that this was the place where Molière first acted before the Sun King; where the Institut gave their reception to welcome Napoleon Bonaparte as First Consul; where only a few years ago the French Government spread a great banquet for Queen Elizabeth II of England and her consort, Prince Philip; and as you remember that feast, think again of the body of Henry of Navarre lying there.

No one has ever known whether Ravaillac was an insane fanatic or an agent of the anti-Huguenots in the Catholic League. In the Place de Grève, now the Place de l'Hôtel de Ville, that Tyburn of old Paris, where the criminals were executed by sword, axe, pyre, rack or wheel, or by a combination of several of these torments, Ravaillac was laid on a platform and torn apart by four horses, each one tied to a different limb and driven in a different direction. But not once under torment did he disclose the names of any who had prompted his crime.

And once again, whoever was finally responsible, murderous violence had achieved only the opposite of its aims. The dagger of Ravaillac, whether or not he was but a puppet on strings, only lifted the name of Henry IV, Henry of Navarre, the Huguenot King, to an honoured place in French history hardly second to that of St. Louis or St. Joan.

7

The Grands Siècles

7

The Grands Siècles

THE great Classical and Augustan ages of France are
the Grand Siècle of Louis XIV, le Roi Soleil, and
the century that followed it, the eighteenth century.
In the case of the eighteenth century, the century of
Voltaire, Rousseau, Diderot and Condorcet, this is true
rather of its philosophy, literature and art than of its
politics, since these were the years when the splendours of
Absolute Monarchy, of the Old Régime, and of Versailles
were going slowly down into death.

Two immortals open the doors and usher in these great
ages of France; they are René Descartes and Blaise Pascal.
Descartes worked his revolution in the ways of thought by
questioning the certainty of everything on earth till he
arrived at one certain thing only, " I think; therefore I am.
Cogito, ergo sum "; and upon this apparently safe and stable
base he began to build. Philosophers, who will question
anything, have since questioned whether it was quite as
safe and stable as he supposed; but, for all that, Descartes
is admitted to be the spring and river-head of modern
philosophy. Pascal was not only one of the greatest
mathematical geniuses the world has known but also one
of the greatest literary geniuses; he is the spring and river-
head of that most clear and sparkling stream, French Prose
Literature.

Suddenly, on a day in 1656, a pamphlet purporting to be
a " Letter to a Provincial " appeared on the bookstalls of
Paris, and doubtless on those we saw on the Pont Neuf.
On the face of it it was no more than a polemic ridiculing
and derogating the ways of the Jesuits, but so exquisite was

the clarity, the precision, the vigour and directness, the satire and wit, of its prose that the days of the " Precious " writers, those who believed that fine writing was a matter of ornaments, affectations, and conceits, were doomed, and a beautiful instrument, French Prose as we have ever since known it, was forged. The prose of the " Provincial Letters," for many more followed this first one, had the lightness of a smile and the strength of a sword. Though polished to the utmost it had all the appearance of colloquial ease. In its attack on the Jesuits and its defence of the Jansenists it could sweep from little eddies of mischievous fun into shattering storms of impeachment and reprobation.

" In sheer genius," wrote Lytton Strachey in his *Landmarks in French Literature,* " Pascal ranks among the very greatest writers who have lived upon this earth. And his genius was not simply artistic; it displayed itself no less in his character and in the quality of his thought. These are the sides of him which are revealed with extraordinary splendour in his ' Pensées '—a collection of notes intended to form the basis for an elaborate treatise in defence of Christianity which Pascal did not live to complete. The style of many of these passages surpasses in brilliance and force even that of the ' Lettres Provinciales.' In addition one hears the intimate voice of Pascal, speaking upon the profoundest problems of existence—the most momentous topics which can agitate the minds of men."

Yes, this brings us to his greatest book, if book it can be called since it is no more than a mass of fragmentary jottings or " thoughts," never finally wrought into logical sequence and shapely form. And yet, broken, tossed and scattered as they are, these " Pensées " or " Thoughts " of Blaise Pascal remain as one of the outstanding books of the world. A chief idea which appears in them again and again is the utter weakness and wretchedness of fallen man, and his greatness too—the greatness that makes him larger than the whole firmament of empty stars, and which could, would he but give himself back to God, attain to a stature beyond the reach of thought.

Descartes . . . Pascal . . . is all the above but words to you, words that perhaps you have often heard? Well, they can fill with life, I think, if you will come to two more narrow streets, not far from one another and both on the Hill of St. Geneviève and there look at some places which no other visitors to Paris (or so it would seem) know anything about.

First the Rue Rollin; it begins with a flight of steps up from the Rue Monge, and indeed it's only a few paces from the Arènes de Lutèce where we stood not so long ago. As you climb the steps the house on your right is on the site of the house where Blaise Pascal died, a young man not yet forty. It was the home of his married sister, Gilberte Périer, and he was brought here in a dying condition that she might nurse him in his last hours. It is in the parish of St. Etienne du Mont and the curé of that church was with him at the end. He wrote that Pascal died " as humble and submissive as a child." His last words, " *Que Dieu ne m'abandonne jamais,*" were a variant of one of the thoughts written in the most extraordinary document he ever produced, which some have called Pascal's " Memorial " and others his " Mystic Amulette."

This is the story of it. A day or two after his death a servant felt something hard sewn into his doublet. He tore the doublet apart and found a folded parchment holding a folded paper within it; on both parchment and paper certain thoughts in Pascal's hand had been hastily, wildly, almost feverishly written down. The servant took the parchment and the paper to Gilberte Périer who later showed it to close friends. It was obvious at once that these words twice written down and so carefully preserved by Pascal, for he had removed them from doublet to doublet, must have had a tremendous importance for him. They seem to be the record of a moment of over-whelming, blinding illumination, which he must never forget, and the record of which he must bear about his person always. This is no place to give the astonishing document in full; but, headed by a rough design of a cross with strokes radiating from it like the rays of a sun, it begins:

The year of grace 1654
Monday 23rd November day of St. Clement
Pope and Martyr and others of the Roman martyrologie
    Vigil of St. Crisogone, m, and others, etc.
From about half-past ten in the evening
Until about half-past twelve midnight
FIRE
God and Abraham. God of Isaac. God of Jacob
    Not of the philosophers and of the wise
Certainty joy certainty feeling joy peace . . .

It continues:

THE SUBLIMITY OF THE HUMAN SOUL . . .
    Joy joy tears of joy
    I do not separate myself from thee . . .
    My God do not leave me
    Let me not be separated from thee eternally

and it ends:

RENUNCIATION TOTAL AND SWEET
Total submission to Jesus Christ and to my DIRECTOR
Eternally in joy for one day of life on earth
(and then in Latin) *non obliviscar sermones tuos*
I shall not forget thy spoken words.

So it would seem that he was remembering, and seeking comfort from, this moment of blinding revelation as he lay dying in the house just here. *Que Dieu ne m'abandonne jamais.*

And that Gilberte Périer read the hastily scrawled record of it in that same house just here.

The Rue Rollin is short; continue along it to No. 14, also on your right-hand side. It is a large house, quite a mansion, and here lived Descartes for some years; here no doubt, pacing behind some of those windows, or, as we know, lying in bed till late in the day with writing materials to hand, he meditated on nature and man and God, and on the chance of certainties in philosophy—long meditations which, years later, having ripened, became his " Discourse on Method," his " Meditations on the First Philosophy," his " Rules for the Direction of the Mind," and upset the thinking of the world.

But more moving than anything in the Rue Rollin is a house in the Rue Monsieur le Prince just across the Boulevard St. Michel. It is No. 54 and the very house where Pascal lived from 1654 to 1662 when he was taken to Gilberte Périer's home to die. Here he wrote the " Provincial Letters "; here, doubtless pacing one of the rooms like Descartes, or perhaps sitting with head bowed forward and chin resting on his fist, like Rodin's " Penseur " he thought and phrased those " Pensées " which because of their vision and their haunting music have come ringing down the centuries to our day. *" Quelle est-ce donc que l'homme! quelle nouveauté, quel monstre, quel chaos, quel sujet de contradiction, quel prodige! Juge de toutes choses, imbecile ver de terre, dépositaire du vrai, cloacque d'incertitude et d'erreur, gloire et rebut de l'univers! "* Great words which were undoubtedly beating in the mind of Alexander Pope when in his " Essay on Man " he set down:

> A being darkly wise and rudely great;
> With too much knowledge for the sceptic side,
> With too much weakness for the stoic's pride,
> He hangs between; in doubt to act or rest;
> In doubt to deem himself a god, or beast;

In doubt his mind or body to prefer;
Born but to die and reasoning but to err;
Alike in ignorance, his reason such,
Whether he thinks too little or too much;
Chaos of thought and passion all confused;
Still by himself abused, or disabused
Created half to rise and half to fall;
Great lord of all things, yet a prey to all;
Sole judge of truth, in endless error hurled:
The glory, jest, and riddle of the world!

" *Le coeur a ses raisons, que le raison ne connait point.*"

" Man is but a reed, the weakest thing in nature; but he is a thinking reed. (*C'est un roseau pensant.*)" Yes indeed; and what a *roseau pensant* was Blaise Pascal.

" Man's greatness is so visible that we can infer it even from his misery. For what is natural in animals is just what we call misery in man. For who is afflicted at not being a king, except a dispossessed king?"

" *Connaissez donc, superbe, quel paradoxe vous êtes à vous-même. Humiliez vous, raison impuissante; taisez vous, nature imbecile . . . et entendez de votre maître votre condition véritable. Ecoutez Dieu.*"

" I see nothing but infinities on every hand, closing me in as if I were an atom or a shadow which lasts but one instant, without return."

" When I consider my little span of life, absorbed in the eternity before it and after it, the little space which I fill and which I can see, engulfed in the infinite immensity of spaces which I do not know, and which know not me, I fall into fear. . . . *Le silence éternel de ces espaces m'effraie!*"

" On mourra seul."

" Par sa grâce j'attends la mort en paix."

*   *   *

Contemporaries and followers of Pascal, in the Grand Siècle, were Corneille, Molière, La Rochefoucauld, La Fontaine, Madame de Sévigné, Boileau, La Bruyère—a great century indeed. But within a dozen years of the century's end the King abandoned his capital, taking his court with him to the palace and park of Versailles; and Paris was royal no more. In Versailles, along its marbled and painted halls, or amid its plantations and parterres, moved the most elegant and mannered society that Europe had ever known; so mannered in its silks and velvets that it seemed to move in a pavane or minuet; but meanwhile in Paris the palaces of the Louvre and the Tuileries decayed. The Louvre standing desolate, the people moved in, bringing poverty and squalor with them. The wide classical colonnade which faces St. Germain l'Auxerrois and the Rue du Louvre was left incomplete and began to fall into ruin. The artists acquired squatters' rights in the long first-floor galleries and lodged and painted there, where now we go wandering among the great canvases of the French, Italian, and Spanish masters. Horses were stabled in the ground-floor rooms. The spacious Place du Carrousel where nowadays we stand to gaze down Europe's finest urban vista—through the Arch and all the way along the Tuileries Gardens and the Champs Elysées, to the Arc de Triomphe on its low hill—this great open Place was then a congregation of houses, hutments, courts, and hovels. And accordingly a pestilent congregation of vapours.

All unknowing, the French Monarchy had gone to the vast and showy magnificences of Versailles to end there its thousand years. It returned to its jilted capital a hundred years later to die on the platform of the guillotine. But in those hundred years Paris, if no longer the political capital of France, was pre-eminently the intellectual capital of the world.

Paris in the eighteenth century was a city fermenting with new, daring, disturbing—and to use the word always applied by jealous Authority to anything it doesn't like— Subversive Thought. The *Philosophes* were taking possession of the city, those writers who gave all their genius to eroding and undermining the whole of the established order with its despotism, injustices, inequalities, and atrocious cruelties. The Grand Siècle of the Sun King had been an age of pure literature; the eighteenth century was an age of applied literature. Almost all its great writing was applied to the enfranchisement of men and the liberation of individual souls from the tyrannies of State and Church. Just consider the names of these applied artists who, though denying the Christian religion from which their fathers had suffered so much, were yet consecrated to the preaching of a new Evangel, a gospel of Reason, Humanity, Freedom, the Basic Goodness of Man, and his Ultimate Perfectibility; preaching it in peril often, because many of them, at the instance of State or Church, had to take their " new thought " with them into the Bastille, the Conciergerie, La Force or L'Abbaye: such names are Voltaire, Rousseau, Diderot, D'Alembert, D'Holbach, Turgot, Helvétius, Condorcet.

For me, as I have told you, their noblest representative will always be Condorcet who, condemned by the Revolution in which all his dreams for mankind, and all the hopes of his brother *philosophes*, seemed to be drowning in whirlpools of horror, sat in his hiding-place in the good Madame Vernet's house and wrote his " Outline of the Progress of the Human Spirit." It concludes with a statement of his faith that men would yet save themselves by reason and slowly progress towards perfection.

If Condorcet was the saint of the *philosophes*, Voltaire was their merry monarch. Voltaire, that subtle and impish old rogue of a writer, was far away from Paris—precisely as far, you may say, as the point of comfort and safety— when at the age of sixty he began his gay and shattering attack on the city in support of the *philosophes*. He had established himself most agreeably in a château at Ferney on the lake of Geneva, which, you may remember, just touches the French frontier, just on the inside of it. Here the bony old man, with a face, save for the glowing eyes, like that of a drained cadaver, lived the life of a country gentle- man, and was pleased with his nickname, The Squire of Ferney. But from this delightful and secure retreat the Squire conducted his campaign, the bombardment of Paris, his native city. The shells that fell upon the city were a rapid series of brilliantly witty and strictly pseudonymous booklets. Lytton Strachey in his *Landmarks in French Literature*, a very perfect essay now published by the Oxford University Press, is so diverting about this cam- paign that I have no heart but to quote him in full. One does not compete with perfection.

" He [Voltaire] had no more time for elaborate disserta- tions; he must reach the public by quicker and surer ways. Accordingly there now began to pour into Paris a flood of short light booklets—essays, plays, poems, romances, letters, tracts—a multitude of writings infinitely varied in form and scope, but all equally irresistible and all equally bearing the unmistakable signs of their origin at Ferney. Voltaire's inimitable style had at last found a medium in which it could display itself in all its charm and all its brilliance. The pointed, cutting, mocking sentences laugh and dance through his pages like light-toed, prick-eared elves. Once seen, and there is no help for it—one must follow, into whatever dangerous and unknown regions those magic imps may lead. The pamphlets were of course forbidden, but without effect; they were sold in thousands, and new cargoes, somehow or other, were always slipping across the frontier from Holland or Geneva. Whenever a particularly outrageous one appeared, Voltaire wrote off to all his friends to assure them that he knew nothing whatever of the production, that it was probably a translation from the work of an English clergyman, and that, in short, one would immediately see from the style alone that it was *not* his. An endless series of absurd pseudonyms intensified the farce. Oh no! Voltaire was certainly not the author of this scandalous book. How could he be? Did not the title page show that it was the work of Frère Cucufin, or the uncle of Abbé Bazin, or the Comte de Boulainvilliers, or the Emperor of China? And so the game proceeded; and so all France laughed; and so all France read. . . .

"Equally effective and equally characteristic is the 'Dictionnaire Philosophique' which contains a great number of very short miscellaneous articles arranged in alphabetical order. This plan gave Voltaire complete freedom both in the choice of subjects and in their manipulation; as the spirit seized him he could fly out into a page of sarcasm or speculation or criticism or buffoonery, and such liberty was precisely to his taste; so that the book which had at first appeared as a pocket dictionary—' *ce diable de portatif* ' he calls it in a letter proving quite conclusively that *he*, at any rate, was not responsible for the wretched thing—were there not Hebrew quotations in it, and who could accuse him of knowing Hebrew?—had swollen to six volumes before he died."

Ecrasez l'infame! This was the cry that echoed again and again in his mischievous writings, and at first shock it may alienate you to hear that the infamous thing to be crushed was Religion—or, rather, and this may be less of a shock, Orthodoxy established and tyrannical. But though no man was ever less capable of a mystical and supernatural religion than Voltaire he was obviously passionately moved by the gospel of the *philosophes*. In a sense he was its St. Paul, writing inspired epistles to the young churches— though with no desire or intention of being " in stripes above measure, in prisons more frequent "; no intention of being beaten with rods, or stoned, or suffering ship- wreck and spending a night and a day in the deep. We must bear in mind that Religion in his day meant intoler- ance, persecutions, tortures. It meant the stake, the block, and the rope. St. Bartholomew was still working towards its end in the minds of men, and not least in that of the roguish and scoffing but secretly humane old gentleman of Ferney. He littered the houses, streets and quays of Paris, not with bleeding corpses but with these booklets whose purpose was to set men free from the fiendish atrocities of which civil and religious despotisms were capable. While he was at Ferney he had heard of a Protestant father broken on the wheel and of two young men, whose offence was no more than making some blasphemous jokes, being sentenced to have their tongues torn out and then be beheaded. *Ecrasez l'infame!*

The last scenes in the drama—or comedy—of Voltaire's life are in Paris. Suddenly, to the surprise of all, he reap- peared there in his eighty-fourth year. To possess these scenes aright you must walk along the Quai Voltaire till you come to No. 27 which stands at the corner of the Rue de Beaune; you must halt there, and after looking up at the house, look across the river to where the Pavillon de Flore stands nobly at the end of the Pont Royal. The ground floor of No. 27 today is a café with tables on the terrace facing the river; but in 1778 this house was the mansion of the Marquis de Villette and here the aged Voltaire, looking like, as I have said, a corpse come brilliantly alive, suddenly on a day in February, after twenty years' absence, appeared with his niece, Madame Denis. Almost the whole city swarmed where you are standing now, and waited here in

the hope of seeing through the windows " *le roi Voltaire* ";
the whole company of the Comédie Française came to do
him honour within the house; every distinguished foreigner
in Paris came to pay his respects to the great man; and the
great man received them all in his dressing gown and night
cap, smiling toothlessly. Now turn your eyes again to the
Pavillon de Flore at the far end of the Pont Royal. This
pavilion is all that is left of the old palace of the Tuileries,
except for the corresponding Pavilion de Marsan on the
other side of the Gardens. It was renovated during the
Second Empire, but, such as it was in 1778, it must have
been often gazed at by Voltaire from the windows of No. 27.
Now, in the Tuileries Palace was the fine theatre with its two
tiers of boxes and its seats for as many as eight hundred
spectators; and some days after Voltaire's arrival at No. 27
his new tragedy, *Irène*, was produced in this theatre with
its author, a frail bewigged old man, sitting in one of the
boxes between the Marquise de Villette and Madame Denis.
The comedian Brizard entered and crowned him with a
wreath of laurel, while the audience stood to acclaim him.
Voltaire, smilingly, happily, removing the crown offered it
to the Marquise, but she responding to the shouted demands
of the people, replaced it on the old man's head. This
famous episode is known as the Apotheosis of Voltaire.

He returned to the Marquis de Villette's house and for
some weeks enjoyed further acclaim and triumphs; he
even, in his satisfaction with these honours, started to
write a new tragedy in this house, sustaining and tran-
quillising himself for this and all the other activities with
strong coffee and, it is said, laudanum. But the strains were
too great; in the middle of May he fell ill and for two
weeks lay suffering here. I often think that surely he
sometimes looked from his window at the Pavillon de
Flore and the Tuileries just across the Seine, and remembered them crowning him there in the theatre, while a
multitude cheered.

As you will read on the tablet above the café, " Voltaire, born at Paris, November 21st, 1694, died in this house, May 30th, 1778." Dying here, he declined the ministrations of the three priests who stood around his bed. *Ecrasez l'infame*. Because of this rejection of the last sacraments and his notorious attacks upon the Church, it was thought no bishop would admit his body to consecrated ground, so it was buried quickly at an abbey in Champagne before any bishop had learned what was afoot and could pronounce his loud " No! "

Those tall windows at the corner above the café's awning are the windows of the grand salon in which he received the great ones in his dressing gown, and in which the Comédie Française played for him; but if you would picture the Hôtel of the Marquis de Villette as it was in his day, you must turn the corner into the Rue de Beaune and see its great gateway still there. Behind the gateway, overlooking the *cour,* is the chamber in which Voltaire died.

For forty-seven years the Marquis de Villette and his successors kept that chamber closed.

Thirteen years after his death, when the year was 1791 and the Revolution was swelling to full flood; when Reason was expelling Religion; when the great new church of St. Geneviève had been changed by the Constituent Assembly into a Temple of Fame; when the name of St. Geneviève had been taken from it and it was called the Panthéon, which is to say a Temple to All Gods; when they had made of it a shrine for the bodies of the apostles of Liberty and carved on its pediment *Aux Grands Hommes La Patrie Reconnaissante,* then they disembodied the dust and bones of Voltaire and brought them to the Temple in a coffin of granite on a chariot of bronze which was drawn by twelve white horses, four abreast, while clouds of incense rose about it, and women dressed in classical modes accompanied it, playing on harps and lyres, and all the town followed—city fathers, ministers, magistrates, foreign

The Arc de Triomphe du Carrousel with the Louvre in the background

Bookstalls on the Left Bank

J. Allan Ca.

Newspaper kiosk on the Boulevard de la Madeleine

Jack Scheerboo

ambassadors, leaders of literature and art. This surely was the real Apotheosis of Voltaire.

We will follow him to the Panthéon.

The Panthéon, whose darkening dome crowns the southern hill as the cupolas of Sacré Coeur the northern, was built as the result of a vow by Louis XV that if with the help of St. Geneviève he should recover from a severe illness he would build for her (and her canons) a temple huge and magnificent to replace her little old decaying church on the top of her hill.

Everything in these days had to be done in classical or Italianate style, and Soufflot, the King's chief architect (His Majesty having recovered), began to raise the strictly Roman temple which we see today, and which, just as it is now, received and swallowed up the Roman Triumph of Voltaire. Its Corinthian portico with twenty-two tall columns is majestic, but its dome above is a failure, being too small and, as it were, too mean, for the ample and tall-pillared drum from which it rises. Before you go up the steps and enter you should walk once round the building, which is in the shape of a Greek cross, and then you will see how in the Revolution they walled up all the windows; you can still mark the difference of the stones in what were the great window spaces, because a century and a half has not yet merged them with the original stones of Soufflot's church; and you will note, I think, how these dark blank windowless walls make the Panthéon look exactly like what it is, a gigantic and domed mausoleum standing, not in a cemetery, but among academic and lively streets on the top of a hill.

Inside it is cold; cold and great and empty and echoing. And again, inside, it looks exactly like what it is, a church emptied of its true heart and meaning. The Panthéon of Paris is the perfect symbol of all that happened in three watershed years—three years which constitute another of

those great divides of history; the years from 1789 to
1791. Begun by Soufflot in 1758 and continued after his
death in 1780 by Rondelet his pupil, it was only completed
in 1789—and 1789 was the year in which the Bastille fell.
At that moment one era ended and another began. By
1791 Religion had been defeated by Philosophy, and St.
Geneviève's new church became this secular temple.
Certainly Religion and Worship have twice been given back
to it, in the First Empire and the Second, but always it has
relapsed. Something has prevented it from enduring as a
church; for the last seventy years it has been the Constituent
Assembly's Panthéon again, and presumably it will now
remain so till the end. It is as if the Revolution in 1791
gave St. Geneviève's new church a wound that was mortal.

It is a sad, then, but profoundly significant place. If you
keep quiet in its huge empty spaces; and it is better to do so
because, do you speak loud, your voice will echo as in a
whispering gallery—if you keep quiet, you may feel great
presences here. They have passed by, and they now lie
beneath your feet, in cells like long clean dungeons opening
from long twilit corridors. The *grands hommes* lie there,
crowned by this last Academy: Voltaire, Rousseau, President Carnot, Victor Hugo, Emile Zola, Marcelin and
Madame Berthelot who died together and lie together,
Jean Jaurès, Louis Braille—some sixty, all told, of those
whom the Fatherland has delighted to honour. You may
go down and see the tombs.

But what will most remain with you, I fancy, as you come
away from the twilight among the tombs, and then out of
that huge, empty, and echoing nave and choir, descending
the steps into the sunny Place du Panthéon, will be the
lovely frescoes of Puvis de Chavannes. These, with their
soft blues and greys and the quiet, statuesque simplicity of
the figures on them harmonise so perfectly with this cold,
stone building. All the other frescoes by other artists—the
martyrdom of St. Denis, and the Life and Martyrdom of

St. Joan—are too harsh and loud in colour for a fane so lofty and white and silent; but look, and look long, at the work of Puvis de Chavanne's soft and gentle brush: St. Geneviève feeding the people of Paris; St. Geneviève watching over her city while it sleeps.

The Panthéon has cast out St. Geneviève; but St. Etienne du Mont stands beside it with her empty sarcophagus and shrine; and the faithful believe that her presence is still there on the summit of her hill, watching over the city; watching over the just and the unjust, over the faithful and the forgetting.

8

The Tumbrils

8

The Tumbrils

1791; and an old world is dead; a new one with much labour and agony is coming to birth. The hour has ignited the fuel and the fuses laid by the *philosophes*; the memory of the Bartholomew and of other pogroms and ferocious repressions have played their part in the ignition; and Paris is on fire; it is aflame with the new ideas, with visions of liberty, equality and fraternity; and the conflagration is such that it will consume many thousands of lives and with its flying sparks ignite other capitals of the world.

Nearly everything in Paris was old when these new visions and dreams leapt up like flames; it was in old and antiquated streets that the new world was born. Paris was still a basin where acres of narrow and tortuous roadways ran through houses whose high walls of plaster, seamed and flaking, rose above archways that led into cobbled and dingy courts. Except for the new quays along the Seine's north bank, I cannot think of a street or road that was not old in 1791; the oldest of all being, of course, those two roads which the Romans laid for their legions and their merchants, one running north and south, the other eastward across the Marais to their provinces in the East.

The present Rue St. Antoine follows this second road somewhat unsteadily; and from medieval times another east–west road met it, somewhat unwillingly, in the neighbourhood of the old Church of St. Merri. This was the Rue St. Honoré, and these two linked roads, St. Honoré and St. Antoine, made up the city's one great lateral artery. You can see from the maps that this artery ran eastward to the Porte St. Antoine and westward to

the Porte St. Honoré. Outside the wall of the medieval
city and just outside its Porte St. Honoré Joan of Arc fell
wounded when she was attacking the gate with her army.
The towered and arched gateway stood over the present
Rue St. Honoré almost exactly where the Rue de l'Echelle
crosses it. (Above the awnings of the famous Café de la
Régence in the Place du Théâtre Français is a high relief
of Joan's suffering face and a statement that the Porte
crossed St. Honoré here; but this is wrong; it is some
yards too far to the east.) A moat lay beyond it, and Joan
lay in her pain on the farther side of the moat, probably near
the spot where now the Rue des Pyramides crosses St.
Honoré. Thus the gilded statue of St. Joan in the little
Place des Pyramides, where she rides so proudly, holding
her banner on high, is well placed and must not be passed
by, as you go shopping in the Rue de Rivoli, without a
thought of her lying there in pain.

In the Grand Siècle and the eighteenth century, with
both of which we have been busying ourselves, the Rue
St. Honoré ran on and out beyond the old strong gate to
newer ramparts, passing on its way the church of St. Roch
and the convents of the Jacobins and the Feuillants, till it
came to a dusty, unfinished and empty road which crossed
it (the Rue Royale) and this led to an enormous open
space, also dusty and incomplete, though it already had
two fine classical palaces on its north side (today the

Ministry of Marine and Hôtel Crillon *cum* the Automobile Club) and in its centre (where now the obelisk stands) an equestrian statue of Louis XV. It was the Place Louis XV; later the Place de la Révolution (and of the guillotine); and now the Place de la Concorde.

The Bastille at one end, the Place de la Révolution at the other—you can see why this became the great road or channel of the Revolution. Eastward along St. Antoine they rushed to the Bastille and overthrew it. Westward along a St. Honoré little different from what it is now, came day after day, evening after evening, month in, month out, those wooden farm wagons or tip-carts called " tumbrils," bearing, not dung to enrich the fields, but men and women, princesses and a queen, Charlotte Corday and Philippe Egalité, Danton and Desmoulins and Robespierre, to mature the Revolution with their blood in the Place de la Concorde.

You want to stand in the Rue St. Honoré and look eastward down its long deep narrow canyon to the blue smoky mist in the distance, and see the tumbrils coming out of it.

Some two thousand eight hundred persons must have come in their tumbrils along this way.

But it was not the tumbrils alone that made this Rue St. Honoré the Grande Rue of the Revolution; for on its north side was the Palais Royal where we shall watch Camille Desmoulins setting the Revolution alight and Charlotte Corday buying at a shop in its arcades the knife with which, fulfilling the stern and proud resolve she had made in her Normandy home, she " touched the heart " of Marat. And farther on, to the west, was the old convent hall of the Jacobins where Robespierre and his fanatical followers in the Jacobins Club inspired and guided the Reign of Terror. Almost opposite the Jacobins, on the south side, was the convent of the Feuillants where the Royal Family was held in bare rooms for three nights after the " suspension " of the King, and before they were all taken to their prison in the ancient Tower and Keep of the Temple. Behind the Feuillants was the Manège, or Riding School, which was the strange habitation and power-house for those controlling forces of the Revolution: the Constituent Assembly, the Legislative Assembly, and the National Convention, which declared the Republic.

So famous was this place that I think you must, for a moment, leave the Rue St. Honoré, by any of the south side roads—only a hundred yards or so—and come upon the new Rue de Rivoli which cuts right across the site of the Salle du Manège. Cross to the railings of the Tuileries Gardens and there on the pillar opposite No. 230 you will see the plaque which tells you that you are standing on a spot which once heard the eloquence of Mirabeau, the loud laughing voice of Danton; Danton's famous shout, *Encore de l'audace, toujours de l'audace*; and then Robespierre's thin, cold voice. If you have imagination you may hear, for a second, these old voices, but then the roaring of the Parisian traffic in the Rue de Rivoli (one-way, and more like a chariot race than anything else), the sounds of English and American voices passing the luxury shops, and the shrill cries of the children in the old garden of the King will sweep them away.

Across this garden, diagonally, on a sultry day in 1792 came the King, the Queen and the little Dauphin, with some loyal friends, hurrying to refuge with the Assembly in the Riding School. The armed mob was storming their palace of the Tuileries. They were given shelter, and from that hour were captives. If you like, you can tread this hasty Via Dolorosa of the Royal Family by strolling, diagonally, through the chestnut trees from the site of the palace to this site of the Manège. Part of your brief walk will be brushed by a children's playground with its merry-go-round and swings and high, laughing voices. *Tout passe*, and in the place of the thorn-trees shall come up the rose.

And so back to St. Honoré.

Only add to St. Honoré the Manège, the Palais de Justice and Conciergerie on the island, and those sites on the southern hill which we visited, and you have the nerve centres and the veins of the Revolution.

Nothing in all Paris is easier than to visit the past in St. Honoré and the Place de la Concorde, for this street and great square are not only the Grande Rue and the Grande Place of the Revolution; they are also the Grande Rue and the Grande Place of English and American Paris. Do not the Avenue de l'Opéra and the Rue de la Paix debouch on St. Honoré; does not the Faubourg St. Honoré with the British Embassy continue it; and does not the Avenue des Champs Elysées come streaming down to the Place de la Concorde? As up on Montmartre, so on these historic pavements, English and American voices seem to reach the ear more often than the native French.

First then the Palais Royal abutting on St. Honoré. It was built by Cardinal Richelieu and here in his "Palais Cardinal" he died, leaving it to the King so that it became the Palais Royal; but in the days when the Revolution was straining to burst all containing bands, in 1789, it was the property of the King's cousin, Philippe d'Orléans, afterwards known, since he took the side of the Revolution, as Philippe Egalité. It was he who built the arcaded galleries about the long rectangular garden, where the jewellers, the cafés, the gun-smiths, the gaming places and the waxworks offered their merchandise or their entertainment to the streaming promenaders, and where the *filles de joie* stood also to offer with sly smiles their merchandise and their entertainment. The long garden was now a popular place for open-air debates and mob-orators, as well as for sitting quietly under the trees in the sun.

It is quiet today as we, the successors of these shades long dead, sit there on some iron seat; so quiet that we can indulge the pleasure of re-creating the past. Who is that handsome girl, in the eastern arcade opposite, weaving so purposefully through the early crowds and looking along the shops for the one her purpose requires? Easy to picture her in feature and colouring for we have her passport which said, "*Laissez passer la citoyenne Marie Anne Charlotte Corday,* age twenty-four years, height five feet one inch, hair and eyebrows chestnut, eyes grey, forehead high, nose long, mouth of moderate size, chin round and cleft, face oval."

Such was her passport, and they let the citizeness, Charlotte Corday, pass. They let her pass, and she has come. And she moves through enclosed shadows because the sun of that day is not yet high above this eastern arcade.

She does not find her shop till she is almost at the gallery's southern end; then she sees it, No. 177, and after pausing a second she walks deliberately in. It is a cutler's, and after a brief time while she is selecting the implement best suited to her purpose, she reappears in the gallery with it wrapped up. It is a sheath knife. She has paid two francs for it, and quickly, among all these people, she hides it in the bosom of her dress.

Her purpose, for which she has come all the way from Caen in Normandy, is to drive it this evening, or tomorrow evening, into the heart of Jean Paul Marat who is hounding her friends, the Girondins, towards prison and death and who has already hounded so many thousand others to the guillotine. Having killed him, she will, if need be, accept

her arrest calmly, for she has come prepared to pay the
price of her deed and to join the victims of Jean Paul
Marat.

That shop at the eastern arcade's southern end is still
there, now occupied by the Ministère des Affaires Cul-
turelles.

Further back into the past—for we shall see more of
Charlotte Corday later on. Exactly four years back, for
this morning of Charlotte Corday's purchase, July 13th,
was, within a day, the fourth anniversary of the storming
of the Bastille. The Bastille fell on the Fourteenth of July.

Let us, then, recreate July 12th, 1789, in the garden of
the Palais Royal.

There are angry mobs in the garden, many of them
debating the King's dismissal of Necker, the " saviour of
France " and the victory of the " Queen's Party " as they
call the reactionary friends of Marie Antoinette, " that
Austrian woman." The Queen's Party, they declare, will
defeat the will of the people in their new National Assembly;
these royalists and aristocrats are preparing a *coup d'état*;
the Royal troops will march on Paris; the hated German
hussars are coming to murder all of us patriots.

It is mid-day, and the little cannon, that "toy" of the
Palais Royal garden, which detonates as the sun fires the
cap, now sounds its loud noon signal. (It is still there, at
the south end of one of the flower-bedded lawns, but it
sounds no longer, and the ivy hugs it.) At the sound of the
signal a young lawyer, a political associate of Philippe
Egalité, rushes out from the Café de Foy, leaps on to a
table under the trees, and in a loud voice which draws the
arguing crowds around him, cries out while he waves a
pistol in the air, " Citizens, I have come from Versailles.
Necker is fled. Breteuil has his place, and Breteuil is one of
those who have demanded the head of Mirabeau." He has
a stutter, and he stammers yet more in his fury. " The
foreign troops are advancing on Paris. The Swiss are in

the Champs Elysées. To arms! Our hour is come. Is there to be another Bartholomew of all patriots? To arms!"

"To arms!" echoes the crowd, for the powder in the keg has long been ready for this match.

"And look!" stutters the young lawyer, whose name is Camille Desmoulins. "We must wear a colour so that we recognise one another. What colour shall it be?" He answers this himself, snatching a leaf from a chestnut tree beside him and thrusting it into his hat. "Let us all wear this for our sign."

The people rush to the trees to snatch green chestnut leaves for cockades in their hats. (I could not find a single chestnut tree in the garden today; they are mostly limes and elms; but this was the origin of the tricolour cockade which succeeded Desmoulins' chestnut leaf.) Then, while some are snatching Desmoulins from his table to embrace him and weep over him, others are yelling, "To arms! Arms!" and rushing to the gunshops in the arcades. These they ransack, and then rush to the arsenals and the Invalides, which they rifle to the extent of some thirty thousand muskets and a few cannon. And so to the Bastille. To the Bastille along St. Honoré and St. Antoine.

Camille Desmoulins has lit, with a stammer, the Revolution. His words in this Palais Royal have summoned from the deeps of men that devil of violence, savagery and blood-lust that lurks always there, never quite dead; sleeping.

Fifty-two hours later the Bastille surrendered. It was then the Fourteenth of July, *le Quatorze Juillet*. The kindly governor, the Marquis de Launay, surrendered it to a deputation from this terrible mob, on the promise of a safe-conduct for himself and his innocent soldiers. They brought him in triumph to the Hôtel de Ville, and in the Place de Grève before it, that traditional place of execution, beheaded him and murdered his soldiers. His head, and other heads, borne on pikes along the streets of Paris, came in time down

the Rue St. Honoré. " *Victoire! La Bastille est prise!* "
Some of Desmoulins' men (and women) from the Palais
Royal had returned with their souvenirs.

All that day of the fourteenth the King had been enjoying
his favourite pastime, hunting in the woods about Versailles,
and, when evening came, he was so weary that he wrote
in his diary only one word, " Rien." Then went to bed.
Early in the morning the Duc de Liancourt thought it wise
to awake him with the news of the fall of the Bastille and
the murder of the governor.

" Is it a rebellion? " asked the bewildered King.

" No, sire," answered the duke. " It is a revolution."

The King did not come in a tumbril along the Rue St.
Honoré to the guillotine in the Place de la Révolution.
They brought him in a coach from the grim Temple Tower
in the north-east of the city to the Place de la Révolution;
and so he came through narrow southbound streets that
only met the Rue St. Honoré where the Rue Royale crossed
—and still crosses—it. The coach jolted onward to the
mouth of the Rue Royale, and those in it who cared to,
must have seen the guillotine. It had been used elsewhere
before but this was the first time it had been set up in the
Place de la Révolution, so it befell Louis XVI, as befitted a
king, to lead the way to a place where some three thousand
of his subjects were to die.

The Temple Tower was a high, square stronghold, keep,
or donjon, with four smaller towers at each corner pierced
by gun-slit windows and crowned by pointed conical
towers like dunces' caps. At first the Royal Family, the
King, the Queen, their two children, and Madame Elisabeth
the King's sister, imprisoned here, were not treated harshly.
They were allotted eight rooms in the Tower and allowed
good food and wine. They were waited on with courtesy.
But later on, when it was resolved that the King must die,
he was not only separated from his family but prevented

from seeing them any more. Then Marie Antoinette in her Tower room could only listen to his footsteps on the floor below.

Poor corpulent Louis XVI, though a weak-willed, irresolute, and helpless king, was always a kindly, well-meaning, considerate man, earnest in religion and loyal to a sense of honour; and in the end some grace and power seemed to descend upon him, some " peace in believing " and some rest in God, together with the memory that his blood had come down to him through thirteen centuries of royal kings, so that he was strengthened to accept all with a quiet dignity and to die like a king among his people, after speaking or writing words not easily surpassed for their gentleness and beauty.

Of an English king who trod this same dolorous road to the scaffold it was written:

> He nothing common did or mean
> Upon that memorable scene,
>   But with his keener eye
>   The axe's edge did try;
>
> Nor called the gods, with vulgar spite
> To vindicate his helpless right;
>   But bowed his comely head
>   Down, as upon a bed;

and except for the word " comely " which fits ill this fat and heavy-chinned man, every word of this might be applied to Louis XVI in his last hours.

From the noble old Malesherbes, his brave defending counsel at his trial, who was later to be guillotined with all his family for this loyalty to his master, Louis heard with a calm dignity that his sentence was " death within four and twenty hours."

This sentence was read to him on Sunday, January 20th, 1793; he bowed to it courteously; and later sat down to write a request for a delay of three days " that he might prepare himself to appear before the presence of God "; that he might be given the confessor of his choice; and that this person might be " sheltered from all anxiety and all fear because of this act of charity."

20 janvier 1793. Je demande un délai de trois jours pour pouvoir me préparer à paraitre devant la présence de Dieu, je demande pour cela de pouvoir voir librement la personne que j'indiquerai ... et que cette personne soit à l'abri de toute inquiétude et de toute crainte pour cette Acte de Charité. ...

He asked also in this appeal to be allowed to see his family before he went from them, and that the Convention would permit them to go free and retire where they would wish. Then, ever considerate, he commended *à la bien faisance de la Nation toutes les personnes qui m'étaient attachés.* Many of them were in need, he wrote, and among his pensioners " *il y a beaucoup de veillards de femmes et d'enfants qui n'avaient que cela pour vivre.*"

This appeal, written with a firm hand but poor punctuation, ends " *a la Tour du Temple le. ... Janvier 1793, Louis.*" Evidently he did not know the exact date—and what a date it was! He had to ask what it was, whereupon he, or another, set it down at the top.

The three days' respite was refused, but he was allowed the priest of his choice and the last visit of his family. The Abbé Edgeworth de Firmont came to him and was with him to the end. And at eight o'clock that Sunday night, the Abbé having withdrawn to an inner room, his family came down the winding Tower stairs to him: Marie Antoinette, his son the little Dauphin, his fourteen-year-old daughter Madame Royale, and Madame Elisabeth, his sister. Four commissaries who were guarding him withdrew like the Abbé to another room but one from which they could watch.

Louis with Marie Antoinette on one side of him and his sister on the other drew the little boy between his

The Hôtel de Ville and Place de l'Hôtel de Ville, the Tyburn of old Paris

Jack Scheerboom

Fishing in the
Seine

knees and made him promise never to avenge him. He
lifted up the child's right hand to make of this a solemn
vow. (" Father, forgive them . . .") For two hours he had
his family with him, speaking to them quietly (so the
watchers reported) and without tears. At ten, it being a
king's royal part to signal the end of an audience, he rose
from his chair. As he pressed his wife to him, she begged
that they might see him again—once more—in the morning.
And he promised, " I will see you again. At eight, before
I go. I promise. Now go."

It was a kindly lie, for as soon as they were all gone,
he asked his guards to ensure that neither wife nor sister
were told the hour of his going. " It will be better so,"
he said. " They must not suffer any more. We will go
quietly."

This last mercy arranged, he went into the small turret
room where the Abbé waited and—how strange it is that
sometimes a weak and commonplace man, with no gift of
language, is granted at the approach of death a perfect
eloquence—he said, " Let me now address myself to this
unique affair."

(If some time you are standing in the present Square
du Temple you are on the site of the old Temple precincts
and within a few steps of the place where the tall Tower
stood, and where the King parted from his family and
then addressed himself to this unique affair.)

All that quiet night in the strong-walled Tower the
Queen lay sleepless while the King, below her, comforted
by his priest, slept well. He was always a perfect sleeper.
Towards dawn she heard the drums about the city beating
the call, for they were assembling eighty thousand soldiers
to line the royal way. No sound from the room below;
but down there, at half past six the King was taking the
Sacrament, his Viaticum, from the Abbé and continuing
in prayer. Sounds of a coach driving up. Sounds of footsteps ascending to the King's rooms. Eight o'clock; he

9—P

had promised to see her at eight o'clock; but no one came
for her. Footsteps going down the stairs. A coach driving
away. Footsteps, yes, but she had not heard, I think, the
impatient beating of the King's foot as he said, " *Partons,*
let us go."

The coach with the King, the Abbé Edgeworth, a lieutenant and two guards rolled through streets empty except
for the soldiers, no one else being allowed on the roads.
The King's hands were not yet bound, so, giving no heed
to the streets beyond the coach windows, he read in his
manual, like those priests in the convent of the Carmes,
the Prayers for the Dying. And so they came to the Rue
Royale, crossed the Rue St. Honoré and saw the Place de
la Révolution. The position of the guillotine on this day
is disputed. Most say that it was near where the statue
of the City of Brest now stands; but engravings almost
contemporary show it near the pedestal from which the
equestrian statue of Louis XV had been removed, and the
Proclamation of the day before states " *entre le pied-d'estal
et les Champs-Elysées.*" What is certain is that it was *not*, as
guides declare, where the obelisk is, but somewhere to the
west of it. The two classical palaces with their Corinthian
columns and pediments (now the Ministry of the Marine
and the Hôtel Crillon) were there to watch the classic
scene; and the architect Gabriel's eight little stone pavilions,
on which later were placed the statues of the cities of
France, stood around at their eight corners.

Let us for one moment halt the King's coach at the
corner of the Rue Royale and the Place de la Révolution,
and turn our eyes to the classical palace at this western
corner. It was once the Hôtel de Coislin, and here on a day
in 1776 Conrad A. Gerard, in the name of Louis XVI,
King of France, and Benjamin Franklin, in the name of
the United States, signed treaties of friendship, commerce,
and alliance, by which France, first of all nations, recognised the independence of the United States. Thus the King

of France blessed the Americans' revolution against their king, and now his coach turns this corner, taking him to die in his own country's version of a rebellion against the king.

The guillotine this morning was encircled by officers on horseback and soldiers standing, many deep, with muskets shouldered. Behind the soldiers there was now a great multitude. The King shut his prayer book, descended from the carriage and, considerate to the end, said to the lieutenant, " Take care of Monsieur Edgeworth." The clock struck ten; the drums rolled; and the King with no halting mounted to the scaffold and removed his coat as if divesting himself of royalty with his life. For a moment he resisted the indignity of having his hands tied behind his back, but the Abbé, who was on the platform, reminded him that his Saviour consented to be bound; and Louis resisted no more. Surely there were ghosts on that platform, or near it: St. Louis; Henry of Navarre. As their descendant was taken towards the plank to be bound to it he lifted his voice as if thereby he might silence the drums and the shouting, and called out, " People, I die innocent of all that men accuse me of; I forgive the authors of my death, and I trust that my blood may cement the happiness of France." Then, when he was tied to the plank and lay prostrate on it with his head ready for the knife, the Abbé Edgeworth, bending down, said, " Son of St. Louis, ascend to Heaven "; and the knife fell. Sanson, the executioner, held up the severed head; the soldiers opened up a path for the people; and they rushed forward to buy from Sanson's valet relics of the King's coat and hair, or to dip their handkerchiefs in the blood on platform and ground. The soldiers marched away, and gradually the fascinated crowd dragged themselves from the Place, most of them streaming back along the Rue St. Honoré to their homes in the heart of the town. It is said that many of them were silent with their heads bent towards the ground.

After the King's coach the tumbrils. They came along
the Rue St. Honoré from the Conciergerie on the island
and met the King's way at the Rue Royale—in this context
so well named. Crowds stood on these trottoirs to watch
them go by, and faces gazed down from many of those
windows at which you glance up now. In the rolling carts
they saw old men, young men, old women, girls, children,
and sometimes, as in the case of Malesherbes, the brave
old defender of the King, a whole family of father, daughter
and grandchildren sitting on a plank side by side. The
carts held any who had been so much as suspected of
loyalty to the monarch, to the old régime, or to some aristo-
crat who had gone to his execution before them.

The guillotine was now set up on the other side of the
Place de la Révolution, between the pedestal and the
winged horses of Coysevox, " La Renommé " et " Mer-
cure," that on their high piers flanked and still flank the
entrance to the Garden of the Tuileries. These are now
matched, on the other side, by the celebrated " Horses of
Marly," at the entrance to the Avenue des Champs Elysées.

Among the first of the famous figures of history to
come this way was Charlotte Corday, on a warm summer
evening after that strong knife-thrust which touched
Marat's heart. A picture shows her standing in the cart
alone, save for the executioner seated behind her. The
picture may be romanticised (for few young women have
touched more poignantly the heart of mankind than Charlotte Corday) but she looks beautiful and pathetic in it
with her hands tight-bound at her back, her auburn hair
falling towards the white fichu about her shoulders, her
head high, her cheeks round and young as a child's, and
her eyes gazing before her, as if she hears nothing and
sees nothing of the taunts, execrations, shaken fists and
derisory pointed fingers of the crowd. The cart is drawn
by a heavy white horse led through the crowd by a man
in rolled-up shirt-sleeves. The jeering crowd cannot get

at her because of the mounted soldiers who ride beside and behind her. It is almost a triumphal procession.

What was she thinking as she came, in some such fashion, along this road? Was she remembering the first letter she had written to Marat from her Paris hotel: " Citizen, I have just arrived from Caen. Your love for your native place doubtless makes you eager to hear of events in that part of the republic. I shall call at your residence in about an hour. Have the kindness to receive me and to give me a brief interview. I can put it in your power to do France a great service." Was she thinking how, turned from his door the first time and the second, she gained admittance to his room on the third because he had heard her voice in the hall? Certainly she recalled that first sight of him in his boot-shaped bath, and how she talked about Caen for a little, how he assured her that all the mutineers she mentioned should be promptly guillotined, and how at that moment the knife swept from her dress and plunged into his heart. " *A moi, ma chère amie?* " Those were his last words of surprise and reproach. " To *me*, my dear? " (The details of this scene at his bath-side are not imaginary; they come from her confession.) Surely she remembered too her proud answer to the Revolutionary Tribunal when its president asked her if she had any reply to so grave an indictment. " None," she said, " except that I have succeeded." Later she declared to the Tribunal, and it could be that she was remembering it with proud justification now, as the cart clattered on: " I killed one man to save a hundred thousand; a villain to save innocents." It could be, also, that she was recalling her last tender letter to her father and picturing him receiving it: " It is only crime which is shameful; not the scaffold "; words so extraordinarily like those which her Queen wrote some months later in the same prison of the Conciergerie.

As her triumphal chariot turned into the Rue Royale,

and after a while the guillotine came into view, she leant
forward to study it. The executioner half rose to stop her,
but she rebuked him, saying, " Monsieur, I have a right to
be curious."

On the scaffold it is said that she placed herself on the
plank and beneath the knife before anyone could force or
aid her there—but the legends of Charlotte Corday are
many, and not all are certainly true. One of the strangest,
and one largely believed—it is often adduced by those who
deny that death by the guillotine is instantaneous—states
that the executioner, when holding up her head to show
it to the crowd, struck it with his fist either scornfully or
frivolously, and that her indignant blood rushed over its
cheeks at the insult.

Three months later another woman came this way alone,
but now the whole long street was lined with soldiers, and
the drums were beating about the city, for this was the
Queen. Not that she travelled as " the Queen " for, as we
know, she made this last journey under the name only of
Marie Antoinette Lorraine, Widow of Louis Capet." We
have a sketch of her as she passed along the Rue St.
Honoré; it is by no less an artist than Jacques Louis David,
the historical painter of the First Empire. He was standing
where the Place du Théâtre Français crosses the Rue St.
Honoré (just by the present Café de la Régence) and he
made this hasty sketch of "the Austrian woman" as she
went by. In it she is seated bolt upright, haughtily upright,
even though her hands are so tightly corded behind her
back; her widow's cap sits high and insecurely on the wispy,
hacked hair; her mouth is turned down and her eyes cur-
tained by their lids as if in scorn of the screaming crowds.
There is no beauty left to the once lovely Austrian princess
except the beauty of contemptuous pride.

The tumbril took her into the Place de la Révolution,
massed with mounted and foot soldiers as for Louis Capet;
while behind the soldiers great crowds stretched away into

the far distances. Led up the steps on to the stage of the guillotine she must have faced, for a last moment, between the winged horses, the Garden of the Tuileries where she had played with her children.

That was October 16th, 1793. Fifteen days later other tumbrils came along with the men in them singing, all twenty-one of them. These were the Girondins who had spent their last night feasting and singing and jesting in that Chapelle des Girondins which we entered after passing through the cells of Marie Antoinette and Robespierre. Now, riding along the Rue St. Honoré for the last time, they raised again the Marseillaise. " *Allons, enfants de la patrie, Le jour de gloire est arrivé.*" And as the crowds yelled up at them angrily, gloatingly, gloryingly, " *Vive la République!*" they shouted back their answer, "*Vive la République!* " When at last they were at the scaffold's foot they all sang their hymn again as, one by one, their companions' heads fell into the basket, so that the chorus got thinner and thinner and died at last with the end of a single man's song.

Do not forget that the Place de la Concorde was the scene of the Death Song of the Girondins.

One woman came along St. Honoré screaming. She was Madame Du Barry. Marie Jeanne, Countess Du Barry, had been a gay, pretty, charming, self-centred and good-hearted young woman; and, reading her life story, one is inclined to think of her as the very Queen of all " good-time girls." One may even think of her as their patron saint, or sinner. Resolved to buy with her fascinations and her favours the best things life had to offer, she began (so it is believed) as a common whore of Paris, rose from these small beginnings to become a famous and fashionable courtesan, progressed further to become the mistress of a count, and arrived at last at a topmost peak when she became officially the wife of a count and actually the mistress of a king. King Louis XV, to regularise, so far as was possible, her life at the court of Versailles, and to give her a name and a title, married her off to a complaisant count, William Du Barry, whose brother had already enjoyed her as his mistress for a little while and, indeed, had recommended her to the King as an article of good value. Immediately after the wedding Count William Du Barry removed himself out of the way for ever so as to leave his countess available for the royal bed. At court she exercised a powerful influence over the King, not interfering in politics like her far more brilliant predecessor in the bed, Madame de Pompadour, but determining the rise or fall of his favourites and often, in her easy-going way, begging him to show mercy to this or that offender under sentence of death. Dress fascinated her far more than politics and she would buy new " creations " for her very attractive person by the dozen, sometimes at the cost of a thousand pounds apiece. Fond of her king and good to him, she mourned his death; mourned too the accession of his grandson, Louis XVI, who had exiled her from the good life at court, and the awful rudeness of his little wife, Marie Antoinette, who had refused to speak to her. Having only a pension now, she came after some years to England to raise money on her jewels, and then, unable in her simple way to under-stand fully what the Revolution, then in progress, was about, and conceiving that she had every right to be partial to the side of the King, she returned to France. At once she was hauled before the Revolutionary Tribunal and accused of having wasted the finances of the State, plotted against the Republic, and worn mourning in London for the late tyrant. Condemned to death, she came along the Rue St. Honoré screaming in an hysterical dismay, unable to believe that this was happening to her—to her who had only been loyal to her master and had never wished much harm to anyone nor sought more out of life than happiness and admiration and fun. In that tumbril she must have passed the shop in this same St. Honoré where, at sixteen, she had begun work as a milliner before passing on (if so she did) to the easier and more profitable work of a brothel. Did she notice it as she went by, and were her cries the wilder for the sight of it? Forced on to the scaffold, she cried, " Oh, you're going to hurt me; you're going to hurt me. Please don't hurt me! " and on its platform she pleaded, " Oh, one minute more, Monsieur Executioner."

Very different the deportment, in tumbril and on scaffold, of another woman, Madame Roland, wife of one of the leaders of the Girondins and, in a sense, their patroness and inspirer. Much of her time in the tumbril she gave to encouraging a wretched, shivering man beside her. At the scaffold's foot she made an extraordinary request that she might first write down "strange thoughts that were rising in her." This refused, she shrugged, mounted to the platform, and looked up first at the knife and then at the huge clay statue of Liberty which they had now erected on the pedestal in the place of the Du Barry's king, Louis XV. To it she uttered the words which have resounded down the years, " Oh Liberty, what crimes are done in thy name." Madame Du Barry had asked that her execution might be delayed a minute; Madame Roland proposed that hers should be advanced a little so that she could be executed before the man she had been comforting and thus "show him how easy it was to die." Sanson, the executioner, snapped that his orders were orders and could not be changed at will; to which she retorted, " Pshaw, Monsieur, you cannot refuse the last request of a lady." And Sanson, perhaps because he was not only an executioner but a Frenchman as well, granted her this request; and she was able to show her friend of the tumbril that it was easy to die.

It is astonishing to read that while this daily butchery proceeded in the Place de la Révolution the social life of Paris, in salons and drawing rooms, was hardly different

from what it had been in earlier years of this brilliant and
mannered eighteenth century. Among gilded Louis Seize
chairs and over dainty Sèvres cups there was wit and gaiety
and cynicism. On the terraces before the cafés, or within
doors around their tables there was laughter and banter
and argument about art, literature, music and politics.
Trade and gossip and argument were brisk in the Palais
Royal's Café de Foy whence Desmoulins had rushed out to
raise the mob to arms, and in the Café de la Régence where
David had stood to sketch the Queen as she passed by.
Carriages and coaches as well as tumbrils passed along the
narrow streets, the gentlemen within them wearing their
powdered wigs and embroidered coats, the ladies their silks
and jewels. " Even though heads are falling like roofing
slates," one man wrote, " we are calm. There are days when
we do not seem at war any more than in the midst of a
revolution." Lovers strolled, their arms about one another,
along the banks of the Seine as they had always done, and
still do; and, though I have not read it anywhere I feel sure
that the patient anglers with their rods and lines were
there, at decent intervals, on or below the quays; for who
has ever crossed the river of Paris without seeing them
standing or sitting on their chosen brinks in rapt and happy
meditation?

Throughout the year of the Terror, from the fall of the
Girondins in May 1793 to the 9th Thermidor (July 27th)
1794 when at last, and in his turn, Robespierre himself fell,
the workmen were completing the building of the Pont
de la Concorde with the guillotine standing in the Place
only fifty yards or so behind them, and we are told that
after a time they hardly turned their heads any more to
watch the too-familiar drama on its small uplifted stage,
but just went on with their work.

Some of the stones which they employed in the building
of that lovely bridge were the stones of the old demolished

Bastille; thus the Revolution is indeed beneath your feet as you cross from the Place de la Concorde to the Left Bank and Boulevard St. Germain.

Much of this shrugging indifference was a symptom of a sick reaction from it all. Now so familiar had the passing of the death-carts become, so routine a business of every day, that the crowds hardly waited for them any more, and the children hardly lifted their eyes from their more engrossing play to see men, women and other children going to death. The reaction swelled, and then many shopkeepers, instead of coming to their doors to see " Barber Sanson " taking his customers to be shaved by the " national razor," put up their shutters in token of sympathy and disgust.

It was the beginning of the end, but Danton and Desmoulins, who had been horrified by the death of their friends of the Gironde, and the savage excesses into which their Revolution, once so beloved, had fallen; Danton, who had wept for his friends, saying, " I shall not be able to save them," and Desmoulins, who had cried out, " It is I who have killed them "; these two, who had begun to plead for some clemency to be shown at times, were now themselves driven by the all-powerful Robespierre to their trial as enemies of the Revolution—or " deviationists," as it would be phrased today.

In the trial Danton, weary of life, " bored with mankind," and ready enough to die, only laughed with his great voice and made jokes. When the president rang his bell to stop this impudence, this contempt of court, Danton loosed a loud scoffing laugh and, turning to the people, shouted, " Do you suppose a man on trial for his life is going to stop for a bell? Oh no! He roars." When sentence of death was passed on him he shouted out, " Infamous Robespierre, you'll follow me! " In the tumbril he stood all the way from prison to guillotine to let the people see him—for the crowds were out again in the warm April evening to see the greatest men of the Revolution following their victims to the scaffold—and when Desmoulins cried to them, " Why don't you save us ? " Danton reproached him, " Leave the wretched rabble there. *Laissez là cette vile canaille.*" Thereafter he joked or sang to rally the others. Desmoulins, who was holding a lock of his adored young wife's hair, may have been thinking—nay, he must have been—of his farewell letter to her, a love letter which almost makes us forgive him all: " Do not call to me. Your cries would tear me apart in the grave."

He need not have feared for her long loneliness after his death; only a few days after it she was condemned on a false charge, went down to her cell in the Conciergerie, sat in that dreadful little hovel where they waited, bound, for the tumbrils, and then followed her beloved husband along St. Honoré " astonishing all by the calmness with which she braved death." Desmoulins' tumbril, coming along the Rue St. Honoré, had to pass the Palais Royal, in whose garden he himself had set this Revolution alight with a leaf picked from a tree.

At the guillotine Danton thought also of his child wife; he was heard to murmur, " Oh my wife, my well-beloved, shall I never see you again ? ", but he braced himself against all such disabling thoughts with the words, "Come, Danton! No weakness." He sought to kiss the man who would go up the steps before him, and when Sanson's assistant tried to prevent this, shouted, " Don't be absurd. You won't keep our heads from kissing in your basket." He, last of all, went up to the embrace of Madame la Guillotine, saying to Sanson, " Show my head to the people. It's worth showing "; but whether he was thinking of his notorious ugliness or of something deeper, a knife stopped us knowing.

One more name we must mention, and honour it as it goes by: the young André Chénier, one of the greatest poets of France, who died on the guillotine only three days before the end. Had he but lived for three days more! André Chénier has often been regarded as a fountain-head of the Romantic Movement, a French half-brother, as it were, of Wordsworth and Coleridge; a French predecessor of Shelley and Keats. But I feel that this tendency to speak of him as a forerunner of these young English romantics derives less from the nature of his poetry than from the fact that his death was so early and tragic, like theirs. One sentimental transmigrationist has even pointed out that his head fell in 1794, and the next year Keats was born. But the inspiration of his idylls, odes, and elegies is not romantic; it is classical and Greek. One true and exact resemblance to Keats he had, in that his poems were " pure poetry," aiming at beauty only; beauty for its own sake, undiluted by any secondary moral or political purposes; leaving " magnanimity " aside, as Keats recommended to Shelley, and " loading every rift with ore."

Like Wordsworth he rejoiced in the Revolution at first because it seemed the end of tyranny and the dawn at last of liberty. " Bliss was it in that dawn to be alive, But to be young was very heaven." But like Danton and Desmoulins he came to hate Robespierre's Jacobins and to execrate the orgies of brutality into which they had forced it. He did not hesitate to express these loathings in poems and prose and, a monarchist at heart, a believer in ordered liberty, he helped Malesherbes prepare the defence of the King. Accused and reviled by Desmoulins, who was not yet converted to similar revulsions, he refused to reply to him, declaring, " It is beneath a man of honour to use his pen against one who can be answered only by denials." He had little doubt that the time must come when Robespierre would order his arrest, and he was in fact arrested at Passy in January 1794 and taken to the prison of St. Lazare. Not till July 24th was he tried before the Revolutionary Tribunal and condemned with thirty-eight others to death. He came down from the Tribunal to a cell in the

Conciergerie (they will show it to you there) and next day the 25th (exactly three days before Robespierre himself trod the same dark passage), as they led him towards the tumbrils in the Cour du Mai, he said to another youth at his side, "I have done nothing for posterity, but—" then touching his forehead "—I had something there." Here is another reason why people like to call him the Keats of France; these words are so like those which Keats wrote to Fanny Brawne: "If I should die I have left no immortal work behind me—nothing to make my friends proud of my memory—but if I had had time I would have made myself remembered."

Danton, Desmoulins and André Chénier died without seeing any answer to their pleas for a return to humanity, but they had thrown the seeds of this on to the winds and it is possible that their death, since they had been heroes of the people, acted as a kind of martyrdom and ripened the seeds. Danton in his remorse had foreseen something like this and foretold it. His last message to Robiespierre was, "I lose my head in the hour when the nation loses its mind. When it recovers it, you will lose yours."

In this he came near enough to the truth. Danton's head was shown to the people on April 6th. Only sixteen weeks later, on the 9th Thermidor, the great things happened; and on the 10th Robespierre's head was shown. The 9th Thermidor in the Revolutionary or " Republican " Calendar was July 27th. The Revolution began in a July; it ended in a July. Both dates are sacred dates to the French, but the first is always known as July 14th, le Quatorze Juillet, and the other as the 9th Thermidor, so perhaps it is as well that whenever you speak this famous name you should remember that Thermidor was the hot summer month, running from the latter part of July to the first days of August, its oddly beautiful name meaning Gift of Warmth. To come at the equivalent date in our Gregorian Calendar, you have to add eighteen days to the " Republican " date; thus the 9th Thermidor is July 27th.

And this was the day in 1794, " The Year II of the Republic," when the Convention itself rose against Robespierre. Since May 9th in the previous year when the Convention left the Manège or Riding School, it had held its sessions in that fine theatre of the Tuileries which saw the Apotheosis of Voltaire and the presentations of his tragedy, *Irène*. The splendid hall had seen also many performances of the Théâtre Français after its actors left No. 14 in the Rue de l'Ancienne Comédie which we visited a little while ago; it had seen the comedies of Molière, the tragedies of Corneille and Racine; but never had it watched a drama more packed with terror and pity than this; never a tragedy more Greek in quality, since here was the Tragic Hero stricken down because his arrogance, his *hubris,* was now more than the gods could stand.

The leader of the conspiracy against him cried to the deputies, many of whom were now afraid lest they too should go the way of Danton and Desmoulins, " There is a chasm deeper than the catacombs at your feet, and either you will fill it with your dead bodies or you must throw down Robespierre and his fellow tyrants." Another conspirator held up a dagger and declared, " If the Convention has not the courage to arrest Robespierre then I shall drive this knife into his heart." He did not need to play the Brutus, or the Corday, for when Robespierre took the floor and tried to speak, that thin cold voice was drowned in shouts of, " Down with the tyrant! " " Death to the tyrant! " He pitched the voice at its highest and cried, " I call for death "; which was met with yells of, " And a thousand times you've deserved it." His young brother, Augustin, bravely put himself at his side—for strangely enough, those who were close to Robespierre in his private life, which was puritan, stainless, and charitable, all admired and loved him; a few others joined Augustin;

but it was useless; amid shouts of, "Death to the new Cromwell" Robespierre and his friends were arrested and escorted to separate prisons. But now the Commune of Paris, which has so often in its history defied the Government, rescued them and took them in triumph to the Hôtel de Ville. Promptly the Convention reacted to this defiance. They pronounced their late prisoners *hors la loi*; the bell of St. Germain l'Auxerrois sounded the tocsin over the city, calling it to arms; and by midnight the Government's troops stood in battalions around the Hôtel de Ville. Their commander forced his way in and demanded the prisoners. There was opposition and a fracas; a shot shattered Robespierre's jawbone, and no one to this day is certain whether the bullet came from a gendarme's pistol or from Robespierre's own, in an attempt at suicide. One of his followers shot himself dead, and the younger Robespierre, trying to escape, got out of a window and with his shoes in his hand crawled along a high cornice. He was seen by the angry soldiers and crowds below and, abandoning further hope, flung himself down. Picked up, still alive, he was carried with dangling, broken limbs to the Hôtel des Barres in the little street of that name behind the Town Hall and the church of St. Gervais. In the end all the wanted men, whether wounded or broken or whole, were taken back to the Tuileries, and thence to the Conciergerie where, probably with unperceived fitness, Robespierre, who was in agony from the shattered jaw, lay for his last night in that cell immediately between the one where the Queen spent her last hours and the Chapelle where the Girondins feasted and sang and waited for their tumbrils in the morning.

In the morning of the 10th Thermidor (July 28th) the guillotine was taken from the Place du Trône (now Place de la Nation) in which thirteen hundred heads had fallen during Robespierre's Terror, and it was set up again in the Place de la Révolution. In the afternoon it was ready, and towards evening the tumbrils came again from the Conciergerie and along the Rue St. Honoré, bringing Robespierre and twenty-one of his adherents—exactly the number of the Girondins, if you remember that Valazé's dead body travelled with them to be guillotined too. After the same fashion the body of Lebas who had shot himself at Robespierre's side in the Hôtel de Ville went along with him to the guillotine. For this cortege the road was massed again with people, and its windows crowded; curses and imprecations accompanied the carts all the way; and it is said that the gendarmes would point to a man in the leading tumbril whose jaw was only held in place by a filthy blood-soaked rag, and say, " Robespierre." Then women screamed at him, " *Scélerat,* go down to hell! Where is my father, my husband, my son? " or, " Go down to hell with the curses of all wives and mothers."

As the tumbrils drew near the Rue Royale, by which the King had gone to death, they passed the door of Robespierre's home through which, only yester-day, that famous and terrible 9th Thermidor, he had issued to go to the Conven-tion and, unknowingly, to death. Behind the blinded windows of the house was a woman weeping for him: Eléonore Duplay, for she at least had been able to love him deeply. The house is now num-bered 398 and much altered; but you can enter the courtyard and see the door through which he came. We stopped the chariot of the King on its way to the guillotine; here at the

10—P

chapter's end let us halt the chariot of Robespierre. This door is one of the many hidden but heart-shaking sights of Paris; you must take your fill of it. Between Nos. 398 and 400 is a narrow passage with a patisserie on one side of it and a coiffeur's on the other. Pass between them into a constricted court and there in the far corner is an old and oddly panelled door, preserved by the City of Paris but known to few. Out of it and into this courtyard he came on that 9th Thermidor, unaware that he would never return through it or that in some twenty-odd hours his head would fall and his Revolution die. It is likely that, staring at *La Porte de Robespierre,* you will not easily come away.

Robespierre died at sunset in the Place de la Concorde where Danton and some two thousand five hundred others had preceded him to death " through the little window." The Revolution itself was beheaded.

9

Paris of the First and Second Empires

9

Paris of the First and Second Empires

THE easterly shoulder of Montmartre, we said, bends round towards the Seine and ends in the slope of Ménilmontant and Père Lachaise. Roughly it is true to say that, as in half the cities of the world, this eastern part is the region of industry and labour, while the western part houses fashion and wealth and comfort.

The place of greatest fascination in the east is the slope upwards through the graves, tombs and monuments of Père Lachaise Cemetery, and this brings us to the Second Empire. Of Paris during Napoleon's First Empire which so quickly followed the Revolution I need not speak at length. All is so well known. Everyone knows that Napoleon, like all dictators and emperors, was a great builder. He would make his capital, he said, the most beautiful city that ever was or ever would be. And do we not see his arrogant " N " on the parts of the Louvre which he completed and on the fine bridges which he threw across the Seine? Do we not see bas-reliefs of his victories on his Arc de Triomphe du Carrousel, and pictures of his battles spiralling round his Colonne Vendôme, with the Emperor himself dressed as Caesar on the summit? We know that he began the building of the great Arc de Triomphe on " the little hill of Chaillot," though it was not finished till 1836, long after Waterloo. He completed the Madeleine, designing it as a Temple of Fame—*L'Empereur Napoléon aux soldats de la Grande Armée*—but he lost heart in it when he conceived the idea of his Arc de Triomphe. After the restoration of the kings Louis XVIII decided that the Madeleine should fulfil its first purpose as a Temple to God instead of to Napoleon; but it was not consecrated till twenty-eight years later, there having been some thought, in the meantime, of using it as a railway station.

It was in Napoleon's day that they began to drive the Rue de Rivoli, named after his victory over the Austrians, right across the site of the old Manège, that storied Head-quarters of the Revolution. Here is a symbol, surely: an arcaded street of luxury shops and hotels, a fashionable " Ladies' Mile," stamping the Revolution under its feet.

Lastly the whole world knows that the first Napoleon lies beneath the Dôme des Invalides. It is the city's noblest dome, and it is fascinating to see how Paris experimented in domes, working its way through prentice cupolas till it achieved this, its masterpiece. First there is the poor and uninspired dome of the Carmes, which watched the massacre of the priests in the garden; then came the comparative failures of the Panthéon on its hill and of St. Paul-St. Louis in the Rue St. Antoine; but thereafter we get the fine dome of the Church of the Sorbonne, the finer of Val-de-Grâce, and at last this lovely thing, the gilded dome of the Invalides.

Towards the Invalides, that home for old or disabled soldiers, the parallel and contemporary of our Chelsea Hospital, the Emperor returned nineteen years after his death on St. Helena. In 1840 the Prince of Joinville, son of the Citizen King, Louis Philippe, arrived in St. Helena, with Britain's consent, to take home the remains of the Emperor. The coffin was exhumed for him, and while he and a few of Napoleon's surviving companions stood around it, the lid was lifted. In silence, but with the old loyalty uprushing, the few companions saw a diminutive figure, well preserved, in the uniform of the Chasseurs de la Garde.

The prince and five hundred sailors took the body back to Paris, and there a hearse " high as a golden mountain " (so Victor Hugo, who was watching, described it) and drawn by sixteen white horses, four abreast, carried the little Emperor between the paraded lines of his Grande Armée and under his Arc de Triomphe which had been completed only four years before—but thus in time for his own Triumph. The Triumph went on—down the Champs Elysées, across the Place de la Concorde, and so to the Invalides.

But the Emperor did not go at once to his present tomb. His body waited in a chapel twenty-one years for the tomb

as you see it now. It took years to find and to bring to Paris the blocks of red porphyry in which, according to the Romans, an emperor should lie. When you look down into the crypt from the marble balustrade under the dome, you see that sarcophagus of red porphyry on its pedestal of green granite. The little Emperor, however, is not immediately within the porphyry; first there is a coffin of oak, then one of ebony, then two of lead, then one of mahogany and then one of iron.

If you go down into the crypt you will see its great bronze door guarded by two giant statues, one of Military Force, the other of Civil Force, and above it Napoleon's words, " I desire that my dust should repose on the banks of the Seine among the French people whom I have so much loved."

Well . . . one can but wonder whether that love was best shown by the sacrifice of thousands and thousands of the French to his own glory and to that of an abstraction, " France," but there is no doubt that his own soldiers thought so and, to judge from this over-magnificent and—

dare one say it?—somewhat vulgar tomb, the good French people were still thinking so when at last, in 1861, they laid him here. And it is their business. Only one looks up at the great golden crucifixion on the high canopied altar and then down into the crypt at the ring of colossal figures representing the Emperor's victorious campaigns—and one wonders if one is not gazing at two polar opposites of human value.

The Second Empire, whatever we may think of the second Emperor, Napoleon III, with his waxed moustaches, his long imperial, his hapless wars, and his lovely red-haired Spanish wife, the Empress Eugénie, was one of the most brilliant periods in French history, at least in the spheres of social life, art, and literature. Its brief eighteen years have even been called France's " Periclean Age." In art it saw Delacroix, Corot, Courbet, Daumier, and the arrival of the Impressionists; in literature Balzac, Flaubert, de Musset, Renan, Zola, the two Dumas, Georges Sand, and Baudelaire; in music Berlioz, Offenbach, Rossini and Gounod; in architecture Viollet-le-Duc; and in building and town-planning Baron Haussmann, whose imprint is greater than any other on the Paris that we visit today.

I suggest that the story of the Second Empire began in the Place de la Concorde. If you will walk southward along the eastern side of that glorious square you will see on the terrace wall of the Tuileries Gardens, just where the wall turns a small angle to lead into the Quai des Tuileries, a lion standing on a high plinth and looking amicably down. Just beyond it, in the angle, there is a small door in the wall. Soon after midnight, in the early morning of February 24th, 1848, out of that door came the Citizen King, Louis Philippe, with his Queen·Amélie, hastening towards a one-horse carriage hardly bigger than an old London four-wheeler. And the lion, if a well-known picture is correct, watched the carriage with something like a smile. Louis

Philippe was escaping from his capital after a revolution of three February days against his bourgeois, middle-class, and well-meaning, but none the less despotic monarchy. Some loyal soldiers still held the square for him, but the crowd rushed forward to engulf the carriage, and one of the soldiers cried out, "Messieurs, spare the king!" The mob obeyed, shouting, "Oh, well, we are not assassins; let him go." And he went. He went to the carriage, the last of the Bourbon kings, the last, indeed, of all the monarchs of France save the somewhat dubious emperor who was about to appear.

I think that Louis Philippe, who meant so well, cast a last look at the Place de la Concorde as the carriage drew him out of it. He had loved it so, and enriched it. More than anyone else except Gabriel, its first architect (who made it out of a dusty and deserted store-ground) Louis Philippe has left his signature on it. He had the obelisk erected where once stood the statue of Louis XV—you can read all about this on its pedestal; he saw the statues of eight great cities of France—Lyons, Marseilles, Bordeaux, Nantes, Rouen and Brest, Lille and Strasbourg—placed on Gabriel's original eight pavilions which, as we told, were there around the square when the guillotine was in its midst.

People clambered on to these pavilions to watch the guillotine at work. What has this vast and noble square not watched? Scenes that Gabriel never foresaw. Besides those scenes which we have already described, it saw, at the beginning of the Revolution, the return of Louis XVI and Marie Antoinette from Versailles to Paris, brought back to the capital in a wild triumph by the hungry, maddened women who had marched out to fetch them and were now waving branches and dancing like frenzied maenads about the lumbering state coach, while their men bore the heads of the royal guards on pikes, often lifting them high for the people to see. It watched, in 1871, the triumphal entry of the besieging Prussian soldiers into Paris after the city had fallen to them. It watched the triumphal procession of the French and their Allies, in 1919, after the Germans, in their turn, had been defeated; and it saw, in 1944, the last battles of the Paris Resistance against these same Germans, retreating once again.

Louis Philippe and Amélie escaped to England, and died there (where Napoleon III would follow them later, and die too). A republic succeeded the monarchy for four years, after which its " prince-president," Louis Napoleon Bonaparte, nephew (possibly) of the great Napoleon, was granted the title of Emperor. The Second Empire was begun, and for eighteen years would be a blaze of artistic renown, social splendour, and popular revelry.

Emperors build. Napoleon III set the Baron Haussmann, Prefect of the Seine, to work on an enormous and merciless reconstruction of his capital. The enthusiastic baron moved immense buildings from one part of the Island to another, like so many sideboards, one such being the Hôtel Dieu which he translated from one side of Notre Dame to the other, across the Parvis; he cut long wide boulevards through the huddled streets—the Boulevard St. Michel, for example, to run in a straight line with the Boulevard de Sébastopol. He drove the Rue de Rivoli into

the Rue St. Antoine. The broad Avenue de l'Opéra is his;
that lavish palace, the Opéra itself, greatly bedecked and
with a huge coronet for roof, can almost be considered
the crown of his work. It is certainly the crown of the
Second Empire. He created the web of twelve fine roads
radiating like twelve wheel-spokes from the Arc de
Triomphe and the Place de l'Etoile. Queen of them all,
queen of all the roads in Paris, was his magnificent Avenue
de l'Impératrice (now Avenue Foch) nearly a mile long
and a hundred yards wide, with its lawns, choice trees and
fine mansions. Fitting that the Boulevard Haussmann
should march almost from the Etoile to the Opéra to remind
you of his name. The Avenue Foch runs straight to the
Bois de Boulogne; and Haussmann, with the aid of special-
ists and the blessing of the Emperor, created this park and
garden of Paris, with its lakes and cascades and chalets
and lawns, out of the ancient forest of Rouvray; we shall
be visiting it shortly in search of famous ghosts who must
surely wander along its sandy rides and bosky glades.

So for its brief golden age the Second Empire displayed
before the world its set-scenes of social brilliance and gaiety.
In the Palace of the Tuileries and at the Hôtel de Ville the
resplendent uniforms of high officers, prelates, and Corps
Diplomatique bowed before, or accompanied, ladies in
gowns of glistening silks, the décolletage of the bodices
being far off the shoulders—for the Empress had beautiful
white shoulders—and the skirts ever widening and bal-
looning till there was nothing for it but to support them on
a steelhooped frame called a crinoline or a *cage américaine*. In
the Bal Mabille on the Right Bank and the Bal Bullier on
the Left, the people who were not invited to these state
occasions, the bourgeois, the marchands, the étudiants
(especially the étudiants) danced and danced among the
gas-lit illuminations hanging from Mabille's fake palm
trees or from Bullier's thousand lilacs in his Closerie des

Lilas. Fine equipages and fine cavaliers spanked along the Champs Elysées, or down the Avenue de l'Impératrice towards the avenues and bridle-paths of this new municipal pleasure-ground, the Bois. Once one of the elegant carriages held the young Queen of England, uproariously acclaimed, with the Emperor riding on one side of the carriage, and her consort, Prince Albert, on the other. In the warm summer nights long pleasure-steamers, brightly illuminated, plied with music and song (as they do still) under the thirty bridges of the Seine.

Famous cafés, all red plush and gilt, came into their own at this time; the Café Anglais, the Café de Paris, and the Café Riche. The demi-mondaines came into their own too: one of them, a Polish Jewess, Thérèse Lachmann, became the Marquise de Païva and built an astonishing palace for herself in the Champs Elysées, all variegated marbles, gilded sculptures, crimson satin walls and painted ceilings, a palace so astonishing that the cynics said, " La Païva has now everything except a pavement on which to walk her beat."

The Païva's palace is there still; it is No. 25 on the south side; but it is almost impenetrable to women despite the shade of La Païva. It is now an Anglo-French men's club, of Pall Mall inspiration, " The Travellers," and only men sit and read, or sit and sleep, among the brocades and the sculptures, or climb the winding staircase of green onyx and perhaps consider the marble bath in which La Païva disported. This predominantly English club is possibly the most comfortable place in Paris, and much of this book was written there, the author sitting, so it seemed to him, in the very bosom of the Second Empire.

So much splendour and accomplishment, so much pride and festival—and suddenly it was 1870. The Emperor quarrelled with the King of Prussia about the election of a Hohenzollern prince to the throne of Spain; he demanded humiliating assurances from him; the King naturally refused and Bismarck, his Chancellor, so altered the King's telegram as to make it offensive to France and to precipitate the war he wanted. The Emperor, vilely advised all through by his ministers, declared war. It was July; July has so often been a *mois fatal* (if one may invent such a phrase) for France. The people shouted with joy at this news of war; they streamed in crowds down the boulevards, singing the Marseillaise and shouting, " *A Berlin! A Berlin! Vive l'Empereur! Vive la France! A bas la Prusse!* " The Emperor had high confidence in his army. The Minister of War declared that France was perfectly prepared and would probably never be so well prepared again. " Should the war go on for a year," he said, " we shall not need to buy so much as a button." And in forty days the war was lost.

Disaster succeeded disaster in those forty-odd days, at Weissenburg, at Worth, at Spicheren, at Gravelotte; and finally at Sedan. Everywhere the French rank-and-file fought with heart-breaking courage, but everywhere there was confusion, doubt, and hesitancy among the leadership, and the war was lost in this rout of Sedan. Sedan cost the French a hundred and twenty thousand men, ninety thousand of them being prisoners of war, the Emperor among them.

Paris, accustomed to military glory, *la gloire,* was stupefied. The surrender at Sedan was on September 2nd. On the 3rd the streets were echoing to the new cry, " *A bas l'Empereur! Déchéance! Déchéance!* " On the 4th, a Sunday, the Legislative Assembly met, appointed a new provisional ministry and arranged for a Constituent Assembly which should determine a new form of government. But even as they were debating this, a multitude of the people of Paris rushed in among them and demanded the instant establishment of a republic. Ministers and deputies, hearing the cry of " *A la lanterne!* " and remembering how the citizens of Paris had hung more than one unpopular minister on the old street lantern at the corner of the Place de

Grève, quickly dispersed. The exalted multitude then marched to the Hôtel de Ville, and there Paris, as so often before, took, or attempted to take, the decisions and the power out of the hands of the national government. It proclaimed the deposition of the Emperor, the end of his dynasty, and the establishment of the " Third Republic." As the young Gambetta, leader of the people, had said to the government of the Empire, " Between the 1848 Republic and the Republic of the Future you are but a bridge, and it is we who shall pass over it." The Empress Eugénie, yesterday the " rose of this fair state, the glass of fashion and the mould of form " (not for France only but for Europe), escaped to Chislehurst in England, where later, on being set free, Louis Napoleon Bonaparte joined her, and there died. Most of his ministers got out of the country too. The Second Empire was dead.

The lost war dragged on, despite Sedan, and the Germans appeared before a defiant Paris. In two days they had completed its investment. Seven hundred guns surrounded it, and a hundred and fifty thousand soldiers. I wish I had space to tell here some of the brave tales of this siege, but I can only refer you to the stories of Guy de Maupassant— seek out especially his " Two Friends "—and those of other French writers, not forgetting *The Old Wives' Tale* of our own Arnold Bennett. In October the Government of National Defence made a tentative enquiry as to the terms of an armistice, but Paris would have none of this. " Never one inch of France's soil to be yielded; never one stone of her fortresses " were the terms of Paris. A poster appeared in its streets protesting " *avec indignation contre un armistice que la Gouvernement ne saurait accepter sans trahison,*" and it is signed " G. Clemenceau." Yes, the old Tiger himself, only twenty-nine years of age then. Forty-nine years later, in 1919, he was to see these disasters of 1870 and 1871 wiped off the slate and a French army marching

through the Arc de Triomphe and down the Champs
Elysées, led by Marshal Pétain, in celebration of its victory
over Germany. His statue stands now on its rock in the
Place Georges Clemenceau, looking towards the Champs
Elysées. Booted and helmeted for war the old Tiger,
Père la Victoire, strides eagerly up the rock towards the
great avenue as if to see this good sight again.

The Siege left few marks on Paris; the Commune, which
followed it, left many. All too many. The Siege, during
which the citizens ate rats and cats and camels, ended after
a defence of four months and eight days. At midnight on
January 28th the Prussian guns around the city spoke no
more. But one of the less bearable terms of the peace
treaty was the symbolic entry of the German army into
Paris, through the Arc de Triomphe of a conquered city
and down its proud Champs Elysées. The Prussians, with
their mounted officers in their spiked helmets, came down
this noble processional route, but all the length and great
breadth of it was silent. The windows of the tall mansions
were shuttered or draped with mourning flags; though
how many unhappy and unloving eyes peered through
shutters, who can know?

The German soldiers be-
haved with decency. They
encamped quietly on the
Place de la Concorde and
on the Champ de Mars, and
on the third day withdrew.

When Paris learned the
full terms which the
National Assembly, then
sitting at Versailles, and
Adolphe Thiers, its "President of the Council of
Ministers," had been forced
to accept—once again Paris

would have none of them. Once again the capital and its Hôtel de Ville defied the Government, assumed the power, and made ready to fight. A " Central Committee " to lead and guide this rebellion, a so-called " Federation," was formed in the city, largely composed of the Mayors of its arrondissements, the officers of the National Guard, and the leaders of its working men.

This was civil war. War between Paris and Versailles. A street poster preserved in the *Archives de France* cries:

REPUBLIQUE FRANÇAISE
Liberté.   Egalité.   Fraternité.
Commune de Paris.
Citoyens, votre Commune est constituée . . .

It declares that the " criminal " Government is plotting to re-establish the monarchy and, for this purpose, begging the aid of foreigners; and it goes on:

> Citizens, you have just given yourselves the institutions which defy all such attempts. You are the masters of your destiny . . . The elected representatives of the People, in order to ensure the triumph of the Republic, ask only that you will sustain them with your trust. As for them, they will do their duty.

LA COMMUNE DE PARIS.

This is the revolt of the "Commune." It brings us to the story of Pere Lachaise Cemetary, where it ended terribly among the tombs.

You must know the whole of this story before you visit Père Lachaise.

Adolphe Thiers, President of the Council, saw that the Commune must be broken at once and the authority of his Government confirmed. Versailles must quickly win its war with Paris. This should not be difficult, because the capital was now alone in its recalcitrance, the provincial cities having deserted it. But there must be no doubt about the victory; the Commune must be pulverised into nothing; and thoroughly, ruthlessly, most savagely, Thiers set about his task. He sent a hundred and thirty thousand men against the capital, and a second siege began. Such an army could not long be held by the poorly equipped Paris militia nor by the city's wild, exalted women who, as ever, marched to the barricades with their " chassepot " rifles slung, yelling the Marseillaise and lifting high their flags and banners which bore the words " *La Commune ou La Mort.*" Versailles forced its entry on May 21st.

There followed the most murderous week in all this long, tempestuous, and blood-bespattered story of Paris. No mercy was shown by the soldiers from Versailles; none by the " Federal " defenders of the Commune. More people died in these seven days than in the six years of the Revolution. All communards found with so much as a pistol in their hands were killed where they stood. In reprisal the Fédérés executed all the prisoners in their hands. On May 24th they shot the Archbishop of Paris and four other priests in the courtyard of the prison of La Grande Roquette. Two days later a hustling crowd, many women among them, conducted fifty-two other hostages—Jesuits, priests, army officers, prominent civilians—to a garden in the Rue Haxo, dressed them shoulder to shoulder against a wall, and there shot them down. (You may visit, if you like, the Chapelle des Otages erected to their memory in the Rue Haxo.)

Before retreating the Fédérés threw down Napoleon's Colonne Vendôme, which lay as chunks and dust on the wide spaces of an empty and silent Place Vendôme, between deserted barricades. They fired the Tuileries, the Palais Royal, the Palais de Justice, and their own Hôtel de Ville, with all its memories. The Tuileries, that storied palace, was riven and shattered beyond recovery, and is no more. The Hôtel de Ville they left a burned-out skeleton; the present ornate building is but a modern version of a magnificent predecessor.

The Dôme des Invalides
from the Place Vaubon

The Tomb of Napoleon,
of red porphyry (as
used for the Roman
Emperors), resting on
its pedestal of green
granite from the Vosges

Jack Scheerboom

Cafés in the Champs
Elysées

Arc de Triomphe

Then with a ferocious and anguished courage the Fédérés gave battle, desperate battle, to the " men of Versailles," all the way up the slopes of the shoulder of Montmartre, up towards the Butte Chaumont, up to the heights of Belleville, up towards Ménilmontant —but ever driven eastward to be rounded up in the cemetery of Père Lachaise. In the cemetery they made their last stand, fighting step by step, back and back, among the huddled tombs,  the white mausoleums, the giant monuments and the temples of the dead. It was Sunday, May 28th, and forced up the cemetery slope, fighting madly in the gathering Sabbath dusk, fighting beneath the May-decked chestnut trees, so that their blood mingled with the blossom on the white tombs, they were driven at last against a wall in the extreme eastern corner, where they died. Against this wall they were shot down, every man of them, even as they had shot down their hostages against a wall.

You will come to Père Lachaise—everyone does—and at the gate a friendly old attendant will give you a paper plan of the thousand graves, so that you may visit—as you surely will—the tomb of Abélard and Héloïse, of Molière, La Fontaine, de Musset, Bizet, Rossini, Sarah Bernhardt, Adolphe Thiers; you will see Colette's tomb and Oscar Wilde's with its monument by Epstein which the Paris police hid for shame (though why?) beneath tarpaulins; but the most fascinating thing of all in this great cemetery is the " Mur des Fédérés," the Wall of the

Federated, now ivy-grown and creeper-hung, in that far, eastern corner. If, climbing towards it, you look back at times, you will see that, from this height, all Paris is visible below you, so that the Fédérés, fighting to death among the tombs and the chestnut trees while Chopin and Balzac and David and Delacroix slept nearby, must occasionally have seen their city beneath them, the Column of the Bastille before which their fathers died, the towers of Notre Dame, the distant domes of Invalides and Panthéon, the chimneys of their factories, and the roofs of their homes. " *Aux Morts de la Commune* " says the wall; and you will certainly see, even at this day, masses of flowers beneath it.

And Adolphe Thiers lies not so far away.

The Commune died against this wall, but because the massacre in the dusk was so savage, a dividing trench of blood has lain ever since between the proletariat of Paris and the Government of France, to bedevil the politics of the country. Every year the revolution-minded people of Paris come to the " Wall of the Federated " to honour the men who died fighting a government. *Hic ceciderunt.*

10

Ghosts in the Bois

10

Ghosts in the Bois

UNTIL the Second Empire the great Rouvray Forest, lying against the western ramparts of Paris, was a wilderness of dying oaks and scrub, a refuge for runaways, a lair for highwaymen, and a duelling ground for gentlemen of honour. Vast acres of it were no more than sapling trees and tangled underbrush, because, after the Battle of Leipzig and the Fall of Napoleon, the British and Russians had made the dreary woodland their camping ground and used the oaks for their fires, leaving desolation behind them. After the Hundred Days and Waterloo the English under Wellington with their Prussian allies gave an exact repeat of this performance; and a century later, during the wintry Siege of Paris, the city's defenders raped the poor violated wood for more and more of its timber so as to furnish their barricades and raise some warmth in their stoves.

The Bois de Boulogne derives its name from our own well-loved Boulogne-sur-mer, that happy port and pleasure-ground just across our moat, the Channel. You may remember that in the seventh century, during the reign of Dagobert, King of France, a little boat drew towards the cliffs of Boulogne. There was nothing in it but an effulgent light and a statue of the Virgin and her child, so it was wafted along by angels. The fishermen of Boulogne were delighted, and, beyond doubt, so were Boulogne's most famous fishwives, but all were a little bewildered till the Blessed Virgin appeared to them in person and told them to make a shrine for her statue on their hill, " as being a place which she had chosen and destined to receive for ever the effects

and the witness of a quite particular cult." Six centuries
later some woodcutters from the great Rouvray Forest
made a pilgrimage to this shrine, and returning to their
village among the trees, raised for themselves a little shrine
like it and called it Notre Dame de Boulogne-le-Petit.
Their village is now a thriving suburb of a hundred
thousand inhabitants, Boulogne-sur-Seine, just south of
the Bois.

The forest remained a devastated place used only for deer
hunts, gymkhanas, and duels till the Baron Haussmann
with his horticulturists, engineers, and landscape gardeners made the desert to rejoice and blossom like the rose.
They turned (to continue in Biblical phrase) the wilderness
into standing water and the dry ground into water-springs
—which is an admirably accurate description of what they
did, since they cleared away the tall weeds and moribund
trees, planting in their stead acacias, chestnuts, pines,
plantains, and fourteen or fifteen varieties of oak; then
made sixty miles of avenues and allées among the trees;
and laid in the midst two lovely sheets of water with attendant waterfalls, the Lac Inférieur and the Lac Supérieur,
feeding them from the artesian well of Passy and the
reservoirs of Chaillot. Working under the enthusiastic
instruction of Napoleon III, they believed themselves to
be creating a replica of Hyde Park, which the Emperor so
admired; we will not disabuse their ghosts, because, after
all, they made a lovely thing.

By 1855, while the Second Empire was still young, the
Bois de Boulogne was the fashionable park of Paris, and
it has ever since remained first in the affections of Parisians
of every class, easily outrivalling the Bois de Vincennes on
the other side of the city and the small internal parks, the
Parc Monceau and the Parc de Montsouris.

I have before me a Galignani's guide, published in Paris
in 1867, the year of the Great Exhibition. At that time the
Bois was still a new joy, and the author so delights in it

that he abandons all reins upon his ecstasy and lets it fairly
romp and bolt through the park.

"Here art and taste," he says, "have conspired to
charm the eye with the most picturesque scenery. At the
southern extremity of the lakes, opposite the islands, two
charming cascades, one of which is now popularly called
La Source, pour their waters, bounding from rock to rock,
or gushing from crevices skilfully arranged into the lake
beneath. Winding paths, emerging from cool fir-groves
scattered around, intersect the rich turf which clothes the
banks down to the water's edge. . . . From the balcony of
an elegant kiosk, situated on a promontory which terminates
the smaller island, an enchanting view is obtained on a fine
summer's day, of the gay scene around. The rich equipages
enlivening the carriage road that winds round the lake;
the crowds of persons of all ranks enjoying the cool shade
on the iron benches provided for their convenience, or
sauntering along the gravel walks; the children frolicking
about in the height of merriment and glee; and the boats
plying to and fro with their white canvas awnings shining
in the sun (the charge is one franc per person) form a maze
of bustle and animation most pleasing to the eye—" and so
he goes on, bounding, one may say, from rock to rock, but
painting, none the less, a memorable picture of the Second
Empire in its gaiety and a very fair picture of the Bois as it
is today.

The lovely enclosure of the Pré Catelan was not there in
his time, at least not as we know it now, with its restaurant-
de-luxe, and its " Shakespeare Garden " and its open-air
" Théâtre Shakespeare." But the weather-worn and
mutilated pyramid, the Croix Catelan nearby at the cross-
roads was there, for it had stood there for two centuries,
and a cross had preceded it since the early fourteenth
century and the days of Philippe le Bel. Thus a monument
has stood on this quiet spot throughout all the political
disturbances and revolutions of six hundred years.

The Croix Catelan has its story: the story of the murder
of Arnauld de Catelan, poet and troubadour from the court
of Savoie. The king, Philippe le Bel, had invited the
troubadour to Passy and he sent a posse of men-at-arms
to escort him safely through the Rouvray Forest, then
infested with bandits and footpads. The bard came bringing
gifts, but, alas, he was given to bragging, as has never been
uncommon in bards and certainly was not so in those
picturesque and gasconading times. So Arnauld de Catelan
had not been walking long through the forest with his
escort before he was boasting to their captain of the fine
treasures he was bearing to the King. They forthwith
murdered him, there on this spot, to come at the treasures.
But, to their mortification, the treasures proved to be
nothing more than a few bottles of valuable essences from
Provence. Disappointed, they returned to the royal palace
and gave out that they had waited in vain for Catelan, who
had not arrived. Search was made in the forest and at last
the searchers came upon the murdered poet's body here in
a copse. The murderers would almost certainly have
escaped discovery, if one of them, a vain soldier and fop,
had not earlier anointed his head with one of the essences,
and this a scent so rare that it was unobtainable in Paris.
Someone smelt the scent—and the crime; the men-at-arms
were apprehended; the guilty ones confessed; and they
were thereupon burnt alive. And here stands the Croix
Catelan.

I never walk along the broad avenues of the Bois, perhaps by the Chemin de Ceinture du Lac, or down the
Allée de la Reine Marguerite and the Allée de Longchamp,
which were the old straight roadways through the forest,
without seeing phantoms under the trees—the ghosts of
the famous who loved to wander here and, perhaps even
more (because the people in fiction can seem better known
to us than our friends) those immortals whom the great

novelists of France have caused to rejoice, or to suffer, in these glades. Generally they have caused them to suffer here, because the great era of Realistic Fiction in France and the beauty of the Bois de Boulogne broke upon Paris at much the same time.

If you are of this ghost-loving humour too, the best time to stroll in the Bois is the early evening, for then, except for the many cars on the straight highways leading to St. Cloud and Versailles, it is quiet and fairly empty. It is deserted because the true Parisian, no matter how he loves his Bois, which is the envy, he thinks, of all other capital cities, does not easily allow anything to interfere with the serious matter of his dinner. It is after six now, and *l'heure bleue*, as Paris calls it, when his proper place is at a table on the terrace before one of his favourite cafés where he can sip his apéritif and contemplate the repast to come. The children too, since it is sunset or thereabouts, have gone with their guardians unwillingly home. Now come into the park by the Porte Dauphine; stroll along its Route de Suresnes towards the Carrefour du Bout des Lacs; and prepare to see ghosts.

Who are these two driving in their open carriage with no special escort but just like the other ladies and gentlemen in their victorias, phaetons or fiacres? The brass and steel of their horses' harness, and the thick glass of their carriage lamps, reflect the red hues in the sky, for it is sunset and their carriage is wending homeward towards the Porte Dauphine and the Avenue de l'Impératrice. They are Napoleon III and his Empress Eugénie, who greatly love this new fashionable Garden of Paris, the Emperor's creation, and like, when the affairs of state allow, to enjoy it as simply and informally as their subjects.

Who is this pedestrian meandering somewhat sadly beside the trees and looking up the vistas to see things invisible to all else? He is a solidly built man with a full-cheeked face, and thick up-brushed hair, and long heavy moustaches; and his eyes have this sad light in them because he is dreading the approach of madness, knowing that it will come. He escapes from this dire thought into the transient peace of creation, and soon he has created one of the most famous of his short stories.

" A Walk " he will call it, for he is seeing, and we may see with him, Monsieur Levas, an old white-haired book-keeper who for forty years has been in the service of Messrs. Labuze and Company, coming to the Bois soon after sunset for a walk before bed. For forty years Monsieur Levas has risen from bed at six o'clock, dressed, made the bed, swept his room, and dusted his chest-of-drawers before going to his office—done the same things day after day, month after month, year after year, because his small salary has never allowed him to marry, and now he seems to have lost all desire to marry or to change his life in any way. He is coming for his walk in the Bois by the Avenue du Bois de Boulogne. (The Avenue du Bois is that same Avenue de l'Impératrice, and it is now the Avenue Foch, for the Parisians change the names of their streets at every crisis in their lively history and on the death of every distinguished general.) Coming down the wide Avenue du Bois Monsieur Levas has seen in the streaming carriages pair after pair of lovers, all embracing in the gathering dark, since this is the time for love. He comes through the Porte Dauphine and into the Bois; and gradually the rumble and the clop-clop of the lovers' carriages die behind him. But under the trees, against the boles, he sees the lovers again, all lost, drowned together, in the sweetness of their embracing and their kisses. There are so many of them.

In the morning a young couple walking in the sunlight along a quiet path in the wood come upon the body of an old white-headed man hanged by his braces from a tree.

" A Walk " Guy de Maupassant will call it, for he loves brevity and simplicity, and he will end with a sentence of typical Maupassant irony. " Death was attributed to suicide from a cause unknown."

Just by the Porte d'Auteuil there used to be, long ago, a pond surrounded by trees and high crowding weeds, on the way through the forest from St. Cloud to Passy. It was called the Mare d'Auteuil, and it now lies on the edge of the race-course, the Champ de Courses d'Auteuil. For my part I can never see it without remembering one Franco-English author who peopled it with ghosts, drawing them for us in his book: the gentlemen in their top hats and neat-waisted frock coats, the boys in top hats too (for they were all gentle people, and very sure of it) and the ladies in flounced skirts and feathered picture hats. This was in the Rouvray Forest, before Napoleon III and Haussmann got to work on it and transformed it into the Bois.

" In those ingenuous days," says the author, " there existed no artificial lake fed by an artificial stream, no Pré Catelan, no Jardin D'Acclimation. The wood was just a wood and nothing more—a dense wild wood that covered many hundreds of acres and sheltered many thousands of wild live things. Though mysteriously deep in the middle, this famous pond was not large; you might easily fling a stone across it anywhere. Bounded on three sides by the forest, it was just hidden from the dusty road by a fringe of trees; and one could have it all to oneself except on Sunday and Thursday afternoons when a few love-sick Parisians remembered its existence and in its loveliness forgot their own."

And there, around the Mare d'Auteuil, according to our author, when Louis Napoleon Bonaparte, instead of being on the imperial throne as Napoleon III was in prison as a Pretender, some of his loyal followers, on parole at Madame Pelé's—the Colonel Voisil, the Major Duquesnois, the Captain Audenis and the Doctor Lombal—would halt with the children, the little English boy, Peter Ibbetson, and the poor little pasty-faced, crop-headed Mimsey Seraskier (destined to reappear later as the tall and exquisite Duchess of Towers) and help them with their fishing.

George du Maurier is far out of fashion now, but if these opening pages of his *Peter Ibbetson* are not an unforgettable piece of the essayist's art, I do not know what is. It is impossible to walk through the Bois today towards the Porte d'Auteuil or to Passy, without thinking kindly of George du Maurier and half seeing amid the trees the creatures of his brain—or his memory.

> *Combien j'ai douce souvenance*
> *Du joli lieu de ma naissance.*

But now a far greater figure comes. It is night and he comes walking homeward and alone through the Bois, where probably he has been dining at one of its more luxurious pavilions. Consider him well: he does not look in the least like a great man, a creature charged with a power to divert, in his own sphere of human activity, the current of things for ever. At first glance you would take him to be no more than a young man-about-town, very much the Parisian worldling, with his high starched wing-collar, his swelling grey cravat, and the white flower in his button-hole. There is even something uncomfortably feminine about that smooth-cheeked face, those large and dreaming antelope eyes, that small and not very successful black moustache under the rich black hair, and—yes, so it is—that slight protuberance of his low-cut waistcoat which suggests a pigeon-breast behind it. But a very great man he is, for his name is Marcel Proust and his immense novel, *A la Recherche du Temps Perdu*, to which he will give twenty years of his life, bringing it out in parts from 1913 till his death, will so affect the order of things in the serious and difficult business of fiction that, as in one of the perhaps greater crises in human history, men will thereafter speak of the pre-Proustian novel and the post-Proustian.

The pleasant opening chapters of George du Maurier's *Peter Ibbetson* are, when compared with Proust's *A la Recherche du Temps Perdu*, like a graceful little yacht, with one man only aboard, sailing ahead of a huge luxury liner filled with half the fashion and wealth of Paris. But, strange to say, those early nostalgic chapters of du Maurier do exactly foreshadow the theme and substance of Proust's great work; the little yacht and the huge liner fly the pennant of the same house.

" And just as when a man is drowning," writes the eponymous Peter Ibbetson, " or falling from a height, his whole past life is said to be mapped out before his mental vision as in a single flash, so seven years of sweet priceless home-love—seven times four changing seasons of simple, genial, pre-Imperial Frenchness: an ideal house, a garden full of trees and flowers, a large park and all the wild things therein; a town and its inhabitants; a mile or two of historic river; a wood big enough to reach from the Arc de Triomphe to St. Cloud . . . all lies embedded and embalmed for me in every single bar of at least a hundred tunes, to be evoked at will for the small trouble and cost of just whistling or humming the same. . . ." What is this but the very text and epigraph for the vast poem which is *A la Recherche du Temps Perdu, Remembrance of Things Past.* Does not any lover of Proust, reading of Peter Ibbetson humming his tune, remember the " little phrase " in Vinteuil's Sonata that recurs through the book, " expressing the Bois in moonlight," and recreating time past, things lost, Swann's love for Odette, Marcel's love for

Albertine? Do not these lesser sentences of du Maurier, which pale before those of the Master, recall some words of Proust's, about the pure air that memory causes us to breathe, perhaps the most famous words he ever wrote: " . . . this air more pure than that which the poets have vainly made to reign in Paradise, an air which alone can give us this deep feeling of renewal, because the true paradises are the paradises we have lost."

How often his " true paradise " is the Bois. How he loves to write about it and to set his characters moving on one of its islands or along the Allée des Acacias and the Allée de la Reine Marguerite. The Allée des Acacias he calls " that masterpiece of beautiful strolling women."

From here onward I shall be quoting from the majestic translation of *A la Recherche* by the late Scott Moncrieff—that astonishing achievement which, in a language so different as English from French, keeps, almost without loss, the poetry, the limpid elegance, and the soft rolling music of Proust's original long symphony in prose, all the qualities which, once met with, make him an addiction for ever.

Scott Moncrieff's translation is published by Chatto and Windus, and I have their consent to present these passages here.

" But most often of all "—Proust is surely speaking of his own childhood, for who is the Marcel of his book but in great measure Marcel Proust himself?—" as I had heard that Madame Swann walked almost every day along the Allée de la Reine Marguerite, I would guide Françoise (his bonne) in the direction of the Bois de Boulogne. It was to me like one of those zoological gardens in which one sees assembled together a variety of flora, and contrasted effects in landscape; where from a hill one passes to a grotto, a meadow, rocks, a stream, a trench, another hill, a marsh, but knows that they are there only to enable the hippopotamus, zebra, crocodile, rabbit, bear and heron to disport themselves in a natural and picturesque setting . . .

" That sense of the complexity of the Bois de Boulogne which made it an artificial place and, in the zoological or mythological sense of the word, a Garden I captured again this year, as I crossed it on my way to Trianon, on one of those mornings early in November when in Paris, if we stay indoors, being so near and yet prevented from witnessing the transformation scene of autumn, which is drawing so rapidly to a close without our assistance, we feel a regret for the fallen leaves that becomes a fever. . . . Into my closed room they had been drifting already for a month, summoned there by my desire to see them. . . . And on that morning, not hearing the splash of the rain as on previous days, seeing the smile of fine weather at the corners of my drawn curtains, as from the corners of closed lips may escape the secret of their happiness—" a typical Proustian simile—"I had felt that I could actually see those yellow leaves with the light shining through them, in their supreme beauty; and being no more able to restrain myself from going to look at the trees again than, in my childhood's days, when the wind howled in the chimney I had been able to resist the longing to visit the sea, I had risen and left the house to go to Trianon, passing through the Bois de Boulogne. It was the hour and the season in which the Bois seems, perhaps, most multiform, not only because it is then most divided but because it is divided in a different way. Even in the unwooded parts, where the horizon is large, here and there against the background of a dark and distant mass of trees, now leafless or still keeping their summer foliage unchanged, a double row of orange-red chestnuts seemed, as in a picture just begun, to be the only things painted. . . . "

As I read that word-painting of autumn in the Bois—it goes on for several more pages, because Proust does not spare his loving readers, but we will rest here, since, as Byron so sadly declared, the heart must pause to breathe, and love itself have rest—as I read it, I see Marcel halted in one of the avenues among the fallen leaves, and with his notebook for canvas, his pencil for brush and his store of bright words for a palate of colours, painting . . . waiting for inspiration . . . and painting again.

He called the Bois " The Garden of Woman," and liked to tell, with all his homesickness for the past, how the Allée des Acacias, planted like the myrtle alley in the Aeneid, used to be thronged by the famous beauties of his day, so that, in the happy hours when he was young and had

faith, he would hasten eagerly to the place where those " masterpieces of female elegance " would be incarnate for a few moments " beneath the unconscious, accommodating boughs."

" Alas! in the acacia avenue—the myrtle alley—I did see some of them grown old, no more now than grim spectres of what they had once been, wandering to and fro in desperate search of heaven-knew-what, through the Virgilian groves. They had long fled, and still I stood vainly questioning the deserted paths. The sun's face was hidden. Nature began again to reign over the Bois, from which had vanished all trace of the idea that it was the Elysian Garden of Woman; above the gimcrack windmill the real sky was grey; the wind wrinkled the surface of the Grand Lac in little wavelets, like a real lake; large birds passed swiftly over the Bois, as over a real wood . . . and helped me to understand how paradoxical it is to seek in reality for the pictures that are stored in one's memory, which must inevitably lose the charm that comes to them from memory . . . Remembrance of a particular form is but regret for a particular moment; and houses, roads, avenues are as fugitive, alas, as the years."

These sentences give the precious essence of *A la Recherche du Temps Perdu,* which bears in its English translation the title " Remembrance of Things Past." Are not the true paradises the paradises we have lost?

Not always do I see him halted in a leafy alley and pencilling his word-pictures of the Bois. I must sometimes imagine him walking the avenues with agonised eyes because he is enduring a torment of jealousy. I say this because it seems inconceivable that, if he had not himself known how terrible, how beyond bearing, the racking of jealousy could be, he would or could have written that awful but deadly precise description of Swann's torturing thoughts, when he fears that his mistress, the faithless Odette, on a day in the past has been unfaithful to him, not with a man but with a woman, on the Island in the Bois. There is no more wonderful description of jealousy in fiction, if indeed there is any to approach it. How Swann is for ever repeating to himself her careless words and charging them with power to lacerate, to crucify, to kill.

" I don't know; really I don't; I think it was in the Bois one evening when you came to meet us on the Island.

" At the next table there was a woman whom I hadn't seen for ever so long. She said to me, ' Come along round behind the rock, there, and look at the moonlight on the water.'

" ' I've heard that tale before,' I said to her; you see I knew quite well what she was after."

In the Bois de Boulogne

Paris *agent* on the Boulevard St. Denis

" My darling "—this was what Swann had said to her—
" It's all over now; was it with anyone I know? "

" No, I swear it wasn't; besides I think I exaggerated, I
never really went as far as that."

But of course it is *not* over now, and it never will be.
On and on he repeats the words, telling himself that they
mean nothing—it is all over now—but then telling himself
that they mean everything, and that he is in a new
circle of hell from which henceforward there will be no
escaping. And the whole awful pattern is repeated in a
later volume with Marcel's agony of jealousy about the
faithless and Lesbian Albertine.

I cannot forbear to end these imaginings of Proust in
the Bois, and these borrowings from his many pictures of
it, without one last quotation, because it holds, for me,
the most perfect of his similes.

" And then, the last carriage having rolled by, when one
feels with a throb of pain that she will not come now, one
goes to dine on the Island; above the shivering poplars
which suggest endless mysteries of evening, a pink cloud
paints a last touch of life in the tranquil sky. A few drops of
rain fall without noise on the water, ancient but still in its
divine infancy coloured always by the weather and con-
tinually forgetting the reflections of clouds and flowers.
And after the geraniums have vainly striven by intensifying
the brilliance of their scarlet, to resist the gathering darkness, a mist arises to envelop the now slumbering island;
one walks in the moist dimness along the water's edge,
where, at the most, the silent passage of a swan startles one
like, in a bed, at night, the eyes and the swift smile of a
child whom one did not suppose to be awake."

11

The Paris of the World Wars

11

The Paris of the World Wars

PROUST *is* Paris in fiction. All his life Paris encompassed him; he absorbed it; he took its colour as an animal takes, protectively, the colouring of its natural habitat.

Born in 1871, just after the end of the Franco-Prussian War, in Auteuil, at the house of his maternal uncle, No. 96 Rue de la Fontaine, to which the family had been, we should say today " evacuated " from the dangerous centre of the capital, he then lived some decades with his parents in the Boulevard Malesherbes, that chestnut-fringed avenue between the Madeleine and St. Augustin. The Prousts' apartment was in No. 9. There followed a few years in the Rue de Courcelles, at No. 45, and then in 1906, after the death of his mother, his father having died two years earlier, Proust set himself up alone at No. 102 Boulevard Haussmann.

Here he lived throughout the First World War, and here he worked in his cork-padded, sound-proofed room, its windows tight closed and its air clouded with yellow vapours which he must inhale, for his chronic asthma and his recurring attacks of breathlessness. Sometimes in the evening he would creep out of the house muffled up to the ears in an overcoat and holding his shoulders high, as if that posture would hold away the night air. He would be going to Ciro's or to the Ritz Hotel in the Place Vendôme, his favourite hotel-restaurant (for he was a rich man) where the waiters knew all his moods and needs. Or he would be coming out to study the Paris sky in these nights of war and to make notes for word-pictures as he had done in the Bois. He noted how the aeroplanes climbed like rockets while the searchlights wandered about the sky " like a powdering of pale stars or moving milky ways," and again " like bright jets of towering water that seemed a reflexion on the clouds of the fountains in the Place de la Concorde."

In 1919, the war over, he had to leave this house with its cork-lined room because it was to be converted into a bank. It is still there but has been so rebuilt and refaced that I cannot recommend you to go in search of it, unless it is to see Marcel coming on to the pavement with his long overcoat buttoned high and his eyes seeking the searchlights that brush the sky above the boulevard. Or perhaps let us suggest that, since you will certainly pass along the Boulevard Haussmann a dozen times during your stay in Paris (as who does not?) you may as well notice the Varin-Bernier Bank, at No. 102, and think for a moment of that vapour-filled room and the black-haired invalid restlessly at work within it, like a hermit crab in its appropriated shell.

He went to live at No. 44 Rue Hamelin, not far from the Etoile, in what he called a " hideous furnished flat on the fifth floor, the exiguous proportions and discomforts of which are only equalled by its exorbitant rent." It was of course in one of the " best parts " of Paris. Here, a gravely sick man, he was cared for, nursed, and fed by Céleste, the young wife of a Paris taxi-driver, Odilon Albaret. Albaret's vehicle was almost Marcel's private car, ever on call, did he want a letter delivered, food fetched from a restaurant, or friends abruptly summoned to come at once for he wanted their company. He soon knew that his work on his novel was a race with death, so Céleste, at the touch of a bell, and at any hour of the night, had to come to his room and take down newly inspired paragraphs at his dictation. Often the dictation proceeded all through the night. Once, in order to describe better the " little phrase " in Vinteuil's sonata, which has so quickening a part in the story, he got the Capet Quartet to play during the night to him alone, while he lay with eyes shut trying, as he told Céleste, to get the impression which he needed for a paragraph. " The impressions I need for my book, Céleste, must be clear cut and unadulterated "—so he lay there on his sofa listening behind closed eyes to the music of Debussy. Surely we may place Céleste Albaret on a humble chair in the Mansions of Fame along with that other serving maid, Rosalie Lamorlière, who tended Marie Antoinette in her Conciergerie cell and brought her soup on the morning that she must die.

Proust was dictating to Céleste till far into the night before he died, and when weakness forbade any more, he said, " Céleste, I think what I have just made you take down is very good. I shall stop now."

I would certainly suggest that you go from the Place de l'Etoile down the Avenue Kléber and, turning into the Rue Hamelin, stand on the opposite pavement to No. 44. There look up at its fifth-floor windows behind which was Proust's " hideous furnished flat." Standing there you will imagine Céleste by his bedside writing all through the night; the Quartet playing Debussy to Marcel, lying alone on his sofa; and the last scene of all, when he died there, with his brother, his doctor, Céleste and Odilon Albaret watching beside him.

Before I leave the Paris of Proust I must speak of a name which recurs throughout his book, the name of no fictitious character but of a real man, living at the time. This is a name which split Parisian society and all France and indeed the world into violently quarrelling factions. Alfred Dreyfus. Captain Alfred Dreyfus of the French artillery who was condemned by court-martial for betraying military secrets to a foreign power, degraded before an army assembled in the cour d'honneur of the Ecole Militaire, his gold lace, buttons, and embroidery being ripped from

his uniform, his sword snapped in two and tossed contemptuously to the ground and himself in this torn and dishonoured uniform marched round the square for the
paraded ranks to see, while a multitude watched from the
Place de Fontenoy opposite; then sent to "perpetual
imprisonment" on Devil's Island, that penal settlement in
French Guiana, only to be exonerated twelve years later,
in 1906, after the ceaseless and selfless campaigning of the
Dreyfusards, and decorated with the Legion of Honour on
the very stones which had felt the fall of his sword and
witnessed his degradation.

All through the publication of *A la Recherche,* from 1913
to 1927, Dreyfus was living in France, and I often think,
did he read somewhere each volume as it appeared, read
again and again the parts that dealt with Dreyfusism—
Dreyfusism in the restaurants, in the salons, and in the
minds of the Prince and Princesse de Guermantes—and, so
reading, thank God that the author was a passionate
Dreyfusard?

Thinking of these things, I went one day in search of
Dreyfus's grave. It is in the Cimetière Montparnasse on
the Left Bank, and much difficulty I had, among those
endless white monuments, in finding it. Maps and plans
didn't seem any help, and at length I asked some masons
and gardeners at work on a tomb where was the grave of
Dreyfus. They stared at me in confusion and ignorance. I
repeated the tremendous name, but their foreman only
shook his head and answered, "*Je ne le connais pas.*" Dreyfus
was forgotten by the workmen of Paris. In the end I found
the grave by wandering from tomb to tomb through the
Israelite quarter of the cemetery, for Dreyfus was by
descent an Alsatian Jew. It is covered only by a flat stone
and bears only the words:

Lieutenant Colonel Alfred Dreyfus
Officier de la Légion d'Honneur

and then the names of his wife and son who were certainly
not ashamed to lie with him there. At its head lay a sheaf
of artificial cornflowers, marguerites and poppies: blue,
white and red, the colours of the flag of France. At its
foot was a small bouquet of fresh roses, gladioli and oak
leaves, which must have been placed there, only a little
while before I arrived, by some nameless person who had
not forgotten.

If you should go to the Montparnasse Cemetery, just off
the Boulevard Raspail, to lay at least your memory on this
flat stone, do not do as I did and search in solitude but
find one of the uniformed *gardiens* who know everything
and are friendly and like to be asked and do not recoil from
a *pourboire* as you shake their hands in farewell. Your
gardien will show you with enthusiasm the graves of Charles
Baudelaire where he lies in the caveau of his kindly step-
father, General Aupick, whom he so despised and hated;
of Guy de Maupassant; of Sainte-Beuve and Saint-Saëns
and César Franck; but I think you will find most moving
of all this tomb which rests above a body once so shame-
fully dishonoured, and thereafter fought over by all the
forces in France of justice and injustice, of hot indignation
and cold laissez-faire, of false witness and race-hatred, and
self-sacrificing allegiance to honour and truth.

The most famous story of Paris in the First World War
is the story of the taxicabs. On September 2nd, 1914,
within a month of the first gunfire, the Germans under von
Kluck and von Bülow, having fought their way with
violence and " frightfulness " through Belgium and northern France, were but fifteen miles from Paris; the French
Government had fled to Bordeaux; and General Galliéni,
left as military governor of the capital, prepared to defend
it once more against the Germans from the old ramparts
that had withstood throughout the winter of 1870-71 the
armies of Bismarck. "*Gouvernement Militaire de Paris,*" cries

an old street poster. " *Armée de Paris, Habitants de Paris,*
The Members of the Government of the Republic have left
Paris the better to give a new impulse to the national
defence. I have received the mandate to defend Paris
against the invader. This mandate I shall fulfil to the end.
Paris, le 3 September 1914. Galliéni." The citizens of Paris,
as ever, took to the barricades. As the Scots to the heather,
so the Parisians, in every crisis, to the barricades. They
built them in their streets of anything they could find:
paving flags, setts, cobbles, bricks. They built them
across the gaps in the *enceinte,* their fortified wall which
still bore the German-inflicted wounds of 1870-71. Then
they waited. The French armies were retreating towards
and behind the Marne, which flows into the Seine at the
very doors of Paris. Foch, in command of the 9th French
army, issued the order, " No one to retreat further. All
must rather die where they stand." His army held; and
Galliéni, perceiving a chance to get behind the enemy
under von Kluck, who had made an extraordinary move
toward the south-east, commandeered every taxi-cab in
Paris and sent up every soldier he could find against the
Germans' flank and rear; Foch attacked at the same time
after sending a telegram, " My right is smashed; my centre
yields; the situation is excellent, and I attack." Von Kluck,
frightened by the arrival of this taxi-cab army, fearing to
be outflanked, retired quickly; and so the whole German
might swung back to the hills behind the Aisne.

Paris was saved, never to fall in that war, and the world
was saved too for a while, by those out-moded, high-
wheeled, brass-lamped taxis. It was a kind of Dunkirk in
reverse, on shore and in taxis. Was Odilon Albaret's taxi
one of them, I wonder.

So runs the story; but when you are next in St. Etienne
du Mont, that lovely little church which holds the shrine
of St. Geneviève on the summit of her hill (and you can

hardly visit it too often) you will find on the wall opposite
her gilded reliquary a marble plaque which tells the story
of the saving of Paris rather differently. It states that when
on September 6th, the Germans were at the gates of Paris,
its citizens " had recourse to their ancient patron " who,
fifteen hundred years before, had by her intercession saved
the city from Attila and his Huns. The citizens came in their
crowds, says the tablet, and prayed for three days before
this, her shrine, till, on the third day the German armies
swung back from the Marne.

Perhaps there is no real incompatibility between the two
versions, since God can only act through men—and maybe
taxi-cabs—as his instruments.

Hostilities might continue for four more years but the
Germans lost the war on the Marne, even as the French
forty-four years before had lost their war at Sedan. Marne
was one of the decisive battles of the world. From the
Marne onwards to the end little happened to leave great
scars on the city. German aeroplanes, Gothas and Taubes,
in raids that were as nothing compared with those that were
to batter and baste France thirty years later, dropped some
six hundred bombs and aerial torpedoes on Paris. In
March of the war's last year, 1918, the Germans' giant
gun, "Big Bertha," opened up on Paris from seventy-five
miles away. In the course of its bombardments it killed
some two hundred and fifty people and wounded more
than twice that number. Its most successful and most dreadful shot was in the afternoon of Good Friday, March 29th.
The fine flamboyant church of St. Gervais and St. Protais
just behind the Hôtel de Ville, was full of worshippers on
this most sacred of days when—the hour was half past four
—a shell from Big Bertha ploughed through the roof of
the nave, overthrowing a column and so bringing down
the stone vaulting, some of it in ton-heavy masses, upon
the people below. When the roar of the collapse ended
and the clouds of dust began to settle, the floor of the nave

was a battlefield with more than two hundred people lying dead, dying, wounded, crushed. Nothing could be heard but groans and cries and fierce execrations where, but a moment since, all was devotion and praise. Fifty-one were counted dead.

If you go into St. Gervais today you can see the legacy of that Good Friday. The restored vaulting of the nave, the restored window traceries and columns, all look as new as if built yesterday, though the shell crashed down nearly fifty years ago. Opposite these restorations is a Commemorative Chapel with a brilliant window shining above the names of the victims. The rays of a great sunrise point towards words spoken on another Good Friday, " Verily I say unto thee, Today thou shalt be with me in Paradise."

It was only eight days before this, on March 21st, 1918, that General Ludendorff, in command of the German armies, had launched their last, tremendous but despairing attack upon the French and British. By the 27th he had driven them back over much of the ravaged land which they had recovered during two years of battles; and on that day he flung twenty-five divisions against eight, stove their front in, and by the 30th was over the Marne. Paris was threatened again, so it is possible that many of those praying in St. Gervais on that day of Christ's Passion were pleading for the salvation of their city. The German drive went on, coming nearer and nearer, and now the people were again in St. Etienne du Mont, praying silently by St. Geneviève's tomb. It was not three days this time but three months before, on July 18th, Foch counter-attacked, flinging all his reserves on to the western flank of the German salient, attacking it on a thirty-mile front from Château-Thierry to Soissons, and a second time, by smashing a flank and seizing a road, drove the enemy away from the Marne. And from Paris. Farther and farther from Paris he rolled the Germans back, day after day, week after week, till at last, in November, they sued for an end of fighting. The end of fighting was denied to them but not a discussion on the terms of an armistice; by the 11th they had accepted the terms, and at eleven o'clock on that morning all was over.

Then the rejoicing Paris crowds packed the wide boulevards from edge to edge, streaming along them like the tidal bore between Severn's banks. Some of them streamed into the Place de la Concorde and surrounded the statue of the City of Strasbourg which for nearly fifty years, since 1871, had been covered with immortal flowers in grief for a lost city; they covered it now with flags and laurels instead and crowned the symbolical figure with a wreath: Strasbourg and all Alsace-Lorraine would be theirs again.

The Second World War did not, as with London, lay whole areas of Paris in ruin. Its scars on Paris were not vast cavities and acres of fanged ruins; they were, and are, pock marks on walls from the bullets of sub-machine guns, empty pedestals in the public places from which the Germans had taken the bronze statues, and, above all, the small square marble plaques everwhere—in narrow streets, broad boulevards or spacious squares—which mark the places where men of the Resistance fell. " *Ici Tomba Heroiquement.* . . ." they say. " *Ici est Tombé pour la Liberation de Paris Georges* . . ." or *Henri* . . . or *Marcel* . . . " *Ici ont été mortellement blessés Jean* . . . *Michel* . . . *André* . . . *Victimes du Devoir et Morts pour la France.*"

In the fearful days of June 1940 when Britain was declaring, through the mouth of its Prime Minister, that, whatever befell, it would continue fighting, " on the beaches, in the streets, on the landing grounds," and " if necessary, alone," Paris, strange as it is to record, was gay and confident. So late as June 12th the *Petit Parisien* was comfortably affirming that General Weygand had a counter-attack ready which was certain of success; but on the 14th the German regiments, heavy-booted and steel-helmeted, were marching in the streets of Paris and over its beloved squares. And this time they were come, not as in 1871 for three days, but for four years. Here was the tramp of the grey army that the taxi-cabs, in 1914, had driven in some panic from the approaches to their city.

France surrendered on the 17th; the Germans occupied all the north and west of France; Vichy governed the " Free Zone," and Paris stood in its vale between its two hills, a crowded and splendid capital without a country.

At first the Germans, governing the city, tried to behave well. They sought (if you can believe it) the admiration of Paris. It was their ambition to transfer any enthusiasm or affection felt by Parisians for their late allies across the Channel to their new conquerors from over the Rhine (Codlin's the friend, not Short). They plastered the walls of the city with posters showing a cowardly British soldier leaping into the sea from Dunkirk and deserting his French comrades; and another showing both St. Joan at the stake in Rouen and Napoleon looking towards France from his place of exile on St. Helena, the caption of which reminded Paris that both these " great national martyrs " were the victims of England. In contrast to these posters proclaiming that the British were thoroughly unlovable there was one (for German humour is often of a somewhat heavy quality) picturing handsome and lovable German soldiers embracing delighted and delightful Parisian girls.

Some Parisians yielded to this propaganda, but not all; not, I think, many, for French wit, as a rule, shoots lethal arrows into all things elephantine and lumbering. Soon behind apparently innocent house-walls the Resistance had begun. And since German humour, at least in the Father-land's military circles, is not such as can stand resistance; since the insolence of resistance to its orders hurts German authoritarian dignity and inflames it, it resorts always, and with a puerile pride in its " strength," to discipline by terror. A German soldier was killed in a Paris street; for

this rebellious act the price exacted was the deportation of
eleven thousand suspect Parisians to concentration camps.
Many of these victims were Jews, for the persecution of
the Paris Jews was now at full pressure. They were now
ordered to wear the shameful yellow star on their breasts.
Many wore it with pride. New posters succeeded those of
charming French girls being kissed by charmed German
soldiers; one said, " The undernamed ROIG, de Paris,
has been condemned to death for aiding the enemy by
recruiting for the army of the ex-General de Gaulle. He
has been shot (*fusillé*) today." In reprisal for attacks on
German soldiers by some Parisians celebrating the anniversary of Valmy (a battle where Germans, a hundred and
fifty years before, had been defeated by the French, and so
a somewhat hurtful thing, even an impudent thing, to
celebrate) one hundred and sixteen hostages were killed.

    And of course the Resistance, instead of being quelled,
simmered to the boil. Such, as ever, is the achievement of
Terror. Any admiration or tolerance which the Germans
had sought and partly won by their early behaviour was a
forgotten thing. The German Power sat like Death in the
conquered city, while from across the water would come,
as we shall tell, the words " *Ici Londres* " and four strong
notes, three brief, one long, beating again and again on a
drum, and promising liberation and victory.

    For a long time the suffering heart of Paris had no true
voice, the Germans permitting no publication of papers
that did not state their case; but at last the wittiest city in
the world found a voice; a voice quiet and pleasant and
penetrating; and this voice was its theatre.

    For much of what follows, and for his translations of
Madame Dusanne's *Notes de Théâtre* I am indebted to
Harold Hobson's book, published by Harrap, *The French
Theatre Today*. A chapter in that excellent book illustrates
well how the rapiers of French wit played with and pinked
the often ponderous German simplicity. In 1940, when the

Occupation was still a fairly new thing, Shaw's *Saint Joan* was produced in a Paris theatre, and the Germans were delighted. Their censorship willingly countenanced it. Was it not the story of a charming French girl driving the English from the sacred soil of France? Moreover, was not its author an Irishman notoriously in rebellion against British hypocrisies and brutalities? Was he not? So they had always heard. To their satisfaction the play enjoyed considerable success, and they permitted the performance of another on the same desirable subject, *Jeanne d'Arc* by Charles Péguy. This they imagined would be even more effective, since it had been written by a young journalist of · Paris who had died in the first weeks of the 1914 war, fighting outside the city—though, mistakenly, against the Germans. *Jeanne d'Arc* was duly produced in 1941; the German officers and men, who were steady and earnest patrons of the fine French theatre, came in large numbers to see it, and they all enjoyed it: did not every speech of the heroine, crying for the ejection of the hated English, draw a wonderfully prolonged and echoing applause? Cheers even. Splendid; and next year, 1942, came Vermorel's *Jeanne avec Nous*—but now, at last, the huge popularity of this subject and play set the Germans wondering. Could it be—could it possibly be—that the Parisians, when they applauded so frantically, were thinking, not of 1429 and the English, but of 1942 and the—

The play was stopped.

Ainsi soit il—but in the same year Charles Dullin, a great man of the French theatre, actor and director both, produced in the Théâtre Sarah Bernhardt, in the very centre of Paris, just across the river from the Palais de Justice, Jean Paul Sartre's *Les Mouches*.

Here let Madame Dusanne take up the story.

"In 1942 a decisive date was marked by Sartre's *Les Mouches*. Sartre had been called up, taken prisoner, and had been returned to France. . . . He had taken an important

part in the Resistance movements of the world of Letters
and of the Latin Quarter. His name, like Camus's, became
a rallying cry for many people who arranged to meet at
his pieces, as others before them had made rendezvous at
the funerals of Armand Carrel or General Lamarque. . . .
Once again (with *Les Mouches*) an ancient story was used to
give undying reality to the contemporary adventure and
prudently to disguise the characters and their thoughts
from the eyes of the censorship. Sartre retained from the
old Oresteiad its essential theme: Clytemnestra giving herself to the murderous tyrant of her people; Electra, the
true heiress, reduced to a hateful and hungry misery at
the gates of the palace; Orestes brought back from exile
by the undying determination of his sister and by destiny
itself; and in the end the final massacre. Orestes had led
afar off a rich and agreeable existence under the supervision
of a fanciful tutor. He came back from happy Corinth into
his sad city, he abandoned peace for murder, because he
could not resist the impulse to be in the bosom of his own
people. He flung himself into alliance with them, exclaiming,
' What do I care for happiness? I want my memories, my
native soil, my place among the men of Argos. . . .' "

And Madame Dusanne continues, " I do not know if
the censorship put down to the credit of Aeschylus this
under-estimation of happiness as a source of comfort, this
deliberate preference for a more ardent life stretched
between risk and action, or even whether it considered it
merely as rhetoric . . . but what is certain is that a whole
generation of youth recognised there its own excitement,
and clearly heard the appeal that was made to it."

Next *Antigone* by Jean Anouilh: produced at the old
and charming Théâtre de l'Atelier, high up on Montmartre
among the trees of the Place Dancourt; a theatre which
Charles Dullin had long made famous. The Sophoclean
heroine, Antigone, it will be remembered, resolved to defy
the command of the usurper Creon that the body of her

brother, who had attacked the city of Thebes as its rightful heir, should not be buried. So eloquent were the speeches of Creon, expounding the need of obedience to authority and respect for edicts and laws, that the Germans conceived this to be a sensible play advocating the collaboration of Parisians with their present masters. And they were the more inclined to believe this because they'd heard that its author had forsworn all politics.

The French were not so deceived.

" What took place during these performances? " asks Madame Dusanne. " Antigone's refusal became the symbol and the sublimation of the personal refusals of all and every- one. Her stubbornness, her 'I am not here to understand, I am here to say no,' may seem inexplicable to audiences in happier times, but they struck to the heart people watched by the Gestapo, and familiar with every misery. And each time she declared or let it be understood that no argument or force would prevent her from returning to bury her brother, the public exulted in its heart, You shall not prevent us from helping the men hidden in the wood behind the farm."

So it was that the Paris theatre contrived, in the words of Dr. Johnson, to " echo back the public voice." It strengthened the secret heart of the Resistance and made Paris ready for its eight great days that were to come.

But there was another voice to strengthen the heart of the Resistance; and this is a pleasing story for us British to read, because this voice was largely able to heal the sore- ness which, wrongly as we must think, the French had felt about our withdrawal from Dunkirk. Daily, everlastingly, monotonously, gloriously, the voice said, *Ici Londres*. It was nearly always a French voice but it came from London, having originated in a tiny room off Langham Place; a *pièce minuscule,* as one of the French speakers called it; a room so miniature that this speaker, so he has since told

13—P

us, used to walk along Portland Place to Regent's Park to compose his script there. *Ici Londres.*

The European service of the B.B.C. had been formed in September 1938 under the shadow of Munich and war. The Section Française broadcast at that time no more than a bulletin of news each evening, and it had but three announcers. Its tiny room was placed between the office of the German Section and the Italian Section, thus, as these merry Frenchmen liked to say, splitting the Berlin–Rome Axis in two. But this little room, this *pièce minuscule*, after the invasion of France in 1940, came greatly into its own. When the situation of the French army was desperate, its front collapsing, and the German tanks bulldozing towards Paris, the German bombers heavily raiding it, and the French Government quitting the capital for Tours, then, on June 4th, " *Ici Londres* "; and France and Paris heard the voice of Churchill, " *Nous irons jusqu'au bout*. We shall go on to the end." And when on the 17th the French Government, under Marshal Pétain, asked for the terms of an armistice, and for France the war seemed to have ended in defeat, there came a new and largely unknown French voice from London. " *Ici Londres* " said the announcer, and the new voice said:

" It is true we have been, and are, submerged by the mechanised land and air forces of the enemy. . . .

" But has the last word been said? Must hope vanish? Is this defeat final? No! . . .

" For France is not alone. She is not alone. She is not alone. She has a vast Empire behind her. She can join up with the British Empire which holds the sea and continues the struggle. Like England she can make unlimited use of the immense industry of the United States.

" This war is not bounded by the unhappy territory of our country. This war is not cut short by the Battle of France. This war is a world war. In spite of all mistakes, all delays, all sufferings, there exist in the world all the means necessary to crush our enemies sooner or later . . .

"I, General de Gaulle, now in London, invite all French soldiers and officers now in British territory, with their arms or without their arms; I invite all engineers and skilled workers of the armament industry now in British territory, *or who may come to find themselves in British territory,* to get into touch with me.

"Whatever may come the flame of French resistance must not be quenched and will not be quenched."

On the day following these words of General de Gaulle the French Section began a new service under the significant title, *Ici la France.* It was a *quart d'heure français,* but its title was soon changed. The B.B.C. had charged a certain Frenchman in London to institute a new programme, and he gathered round himself a small team of broadcasters who should express the true thoughts and hopes— and nothing else—of the people in a France and a Paris which had fallen. He had only five at first: Jean Martin, Pierre Bourdan, Jean Oberlé, Jacques Borel, and Maurice Van Moppès. Some of these names are *noms de guerre* (apt description for once); it was unwise to speak from London under your true name if you had a family in France.

The founder of the team took the *nom de guerre* of Jacques Duchesne. He was Michel St. Denis, creator of the Compagnie des Quinze, and a theatrical producer hardly more celebrated in Paris than in London.

With his five friends he began the famous French half-hour which later took the title, *Les Français Parlent aux Français* and endured for four and a half years. It was a pleasant programme—not seldom containing, amid the wit, its code instructions to the Resistance.

From the first these Frenchmen insisted on speaking only the exact truth to their countrymen. Useless, they said, to speak happy things or unjustified hopes to a France which knew its own unhappiness and was quick, as ever, to prick all balloons of exaggeration and lies. They must echo back the *true* public voice of their country and capital, and they did not hesitate to say at times, " *Aujourd'hui les nouvelles sont mauvaises.*" It was their way of offering to their people, for the present, only blood and toil, sweat and tears. The B.B.C. was at one with them in this; in the early days of the war it had made the mistake, more than once, of exaggerating successes and minimising defeats, but it had learnt its lesson. Only the truth, however unpalatable, must be spoken; only such hopes as could be sincerely held. Wonderful was the result. While Radio Paris and all other French stations under enemy control were pouring out, in the names of propaganda and war, their lies, calumnies and cheap, easy insults, the French, ever clear-eyed, hard-headed, and cynical, would close their windows and shutters (those familiar shutters of all the long Paris streets) and lower their sets and listen to a voice which said, " *Ici Londres.*"

" *Ici Londres. Attention! Baissez vos postes s'il y a lieu.* Lower your sets if it's necessary. The evening newspaper, *Evening Standard,* which appears in London, devoted its editorial of last Tuesday to France at War. Here is a translation of this article . . .*"

And so on, till the broadcast ended, " *Ici Londres. Ceci terminé notre programme français. Bon soir, Mesdames. Bon soir, Mesdemoiselles. Bon soir, Messieurs.*" And the music of London burst into the Sambre et Meuse March. Or the Marseillaise.

There was a quarter of an hour for the French children too. On Thursday afternoons because this day was their half-holiday.

Ici Londres. Voici le quart d'heure des petits enfants de France. No propaganda followed; only stories and small plays; only something to let the children of Occupied France know that the Free French in London—later to be called the Fighting French—had not forgotten them. " *Ecoutez la légende du Minotaure. . . . Et maintenant voici un conte, La Cloche du Roi. . . .*" And so on to the close, "*Voici terminé votre quart d'heure de jeudi après-midi. Au revoir, chers petits enfants de France. Au revoir.*"

In 1941 and '42 the Resistance was hardening into activity, and the French Service broadcast many slogans and easy rhythmic rhymes for their use, their encouragement, or their diversion. One day, gently, Jean Oberlé hummed:

> *Radio Paris ment* (Radio Paris lies)
> *Radio Paris ment*
> *Radio Paris est allemand* (Radio Paris is German)

and soon all Parisians were humming the awful rhythm and adding a last line of their own, *Mais ce n'est pas pour longtemps.*

After the sinking of Mussolini's battleships in the port of Taranto, a suave voice offered the French a parody of one of Chénier's lyrics:

> *Pleurez, pauvre Musso, o vous sacré Duce*
> *Duce cher à Ciano, pauvre Musso, pleurez.*

And later, when good accounts of the Resistance were being received in London, a voice sang in the soft delicate but mischievous fashion of, say, Maurice Chevalier or Jean Sablon:

> *Il ne faut pas*
> *Désespérer*
> *On les aura!*
> (the famous slogan of the first war, " We shall *get* them! ")
> *Il ne faut pas*
> *Vous arrêter*
> *De résister*

Meantime—in January 1941—had come the most brilliantly successful stratagem of all: the V sign. You may say that it was the gamins, the naughtier boys (and, I hope,

the gamines too) of Occupied Brussels who started it;
those who chalk up their graffiti on all inviting street walls.
In peacetime they had probably, like their peers in England,
contented themselves with blazoning news of merely local
interest, such as " Gaston loves Renée "; now, their view
enlarging to match heroic days, they just chalked up R.A.F.
to annoy their German masters. Two excellent speakers
of the B.B.C.'s Radio Belge, a M. Victor de Laveleye and
a M. Naud Geersens felt that this infantile behaviour of
their young compatriots should be encouraged, and, con-
sidering the matter as fully as it deserved, came to the
conclusion that these and other scrawlers-on-walls should
be given an easier symbol with which to chafe and dis-
compose the Germans; not three rather elaborate letters,
R.A.F., but one; one small and very simple; one that had
the least possible number of strokes; one that could be
inscribed before any German policeman could see what
was toward—in short, what you might call a quick-and-run
sign. And in some moment when a star danced they
thought of the letter V. V, which would stand for " Victory " and " *Victoire* " and the Flemish " *Vrijheid* (Liberty)."

And on January 14th M. de Laveleye went on the air as
follows:

" It is necessary that all Belgian patriots should have a
rallying sign; that they should multiply this sign around
them; that, seeing it inscribed everywhere, they may know
themselves for a multitude; and that the German Occupier,
he also, in seeing this symbol always the same and inde-
finitely repeated, may know that he is surrounded, hemmed
in, by an innumerable multitude of citizens who wait
impatiently, and watch impatiently, for the first sign of his
weakening."

Whereupon he announced the V sign, and explained it.

Instantly almost every available wall in Belgium bore
the V. And the rash did not stop there. Before the B.B.C.
could propose to France a similar campaign the V was

everywhere on the walls of Paris, and not in Paris only but in all France—nay, over much of Occupied Europe—so many were the people who listened to *la bibici* speaking in a tongue they understood.

The Germans reacted to this " child's-play " (*enfantillage*) with warnings, threats, fines, and imprisonments, but the V went ever on the walls, and sometimes if no policeman was about, it was joined by R.A.F., for good measure. Meanwhile from the B.B.C. in London a mysterious " Colonel Britton " was encouraging his continent-wide army of daubers with regular offerings of commendation and instruction. No one knew who he was; no one was allowed to know. And on June 27th he announced " the V sign in sound." He reminded his listeners that Morse signallers tapped out the letter V with three shorts and a long. He explained also that this " V in sound " could be written—on walls, perhaps?—on trottoirs?—as three dots and a dash. Such a sign in fact as he who runs may write.

Immediately, all over Paris (all over Europe too, but Paris is our subject) the three dots and a dash appeared on the walls in chalk, or whitewash, or good white paint; for no one can surpass the burgesses of Paris in this business of inscribing their political sentiments on walls.

Next the B.B.C., doubtless uplifted by this *succès fou*, began to use the same four Morse beats, on a drum, for their interval signal. Every twenty seconds the drum tapped its V to Europe—and this history-laden tapping has remained their interval signal in the European service ever since. Further *la bibici* had a cock whose cocorico was three shorts and a long; a dog which barked to the same measure; and a clock which did not fail to emphasise that five o'clock in Roman numerals was a V. And ever and again the great four opening chords of Beethoven's " Fifth Symphony " hammered at Europe—" Fate Knocking at the Door."

In Paris when a German, or Germans, passed along the
trottoirs, the tables on the café terraces resounded gently
with taps, three gentle, one less so; inside the restaurants,
did some German come in for a good French-cooked meal,
the tables became softly zylophonic too, and the waiters
in their white jackets rattled their trays (by accident?) three
times and a fourth; in the theatres—and the Germans, as
we have told, enjoyed the Paris theatres—or they did up
till now—the French audience, at curtain fall, applauded
vigorously, and in unison, with the V sign in sound. Was
the play a bore, someone would cough, three soft coughs
and one hearty. An example that, likely enough, was followed in other parts of the house.

Dr. Goebbels and his Ministry of Propaganda, vexed,
unhappy, and at last gravely disturbed, tried to counter
this V, which was sniping at them everywhere, by asserting
that it could stand for *Viktoria,* a rallying sign for all who
would fight Bolshevism; they even had it painted on their
lorries, tanks, and cars. And all who know the Parisians
can imagine with what ridicule this attempt was greeted.
The café tables rapped a welcome as a German V went by;
window panes tapped a tatta-tattoo; and rude boys whistled
the Fifth Symphony.

It will be enough, perhaps, to look at two houses in
Paris and, staring up at their windows and shutters, to
imagine the secret workings of the Resistance, and its
heroisms. One of these, oddly enough, we have considered
already in a different context. It is none other than the
house on the Quai Voltaire, No. 27, where Voltaire died
after his apotheosis just across the river in the theatre of
the Tuileries. In his day, when it was the home of the
Marquis de Villette, it had known the discussions and the
conspiracies of the revolutionaries, Desmoulins, Condorcet,
Montesquieu and others; now the plaques on its wall tell
us that, not only did it see the death of Voltaire, but that it

From the Quai du Louvre looking towards the Pont des Arts and the Ile de la Cité

Hôtel de Ville in foreground, St. Gervais behind; with the Ile St. Louis on the right

Artists on the Ile
St. Louis

Walter Kirchberger

Autumn in the Luxembourg Gardens, showing in the background the
Palais du Luxembourg, home since 1946 of the Conseil de la République

was a place of meeting of the leaders of the Resistance. This subsequent history would not, I think, have disquieted that poor emaciated cadaver, the dying Voltaire.

The other house is a large mansion in a most fashionable part of Paris, No. 42, in the Rue Bassano, not many steps from the Avenue des Champs Elysées. The plaque tells its story in words to which I will add nothing: *En Hommage aux Resistants Torturés dans cette Maison pendant l'Occupation, 1940–1944.*"

Then come to the city's centre, the Place du Parvis Notre Dame, on the central Island. This is truly the centre of the city since all the great roads of France radiating from the capital measure their length from here. It was fitting, therefore, that the Resistance should have risen from its subterranean activity and come into open battle here with the city's masters. Facing Notre Dame across the large square is the Préfecture de Police; and on August 19th, 1944, summoned to action by the army of General Leclerc advancing to the city's liberation, the police struck work and, fortifying themselves in this stout old nineteenth-century barrack, challenged the Germans to do their worst. Walk along the front of the Hôtel Dieu, which stretches from the Préfecture to the Cathedral, and you will see all along it plaques marking the spots where *gardiens de la paix* fell in a street battle. By the position of these plaques you can imagine a running fight. Turn the corner of the Préfecture on to the Quai du Marché Neuf and look at once on the wall of the Préfecture facing the river. Here a large commemorative stone says:

Ici fut reçu
Le 24 Août 1944
d'un avion léger
De la 2ᵉ Division Blindée
Le Message du Général Leclerc
Aux Parisiens Combatants

" TENEZ BONS NOUS ARRIVONS "
Lancé
Par le Capitaine Jean Collet
et par
Le Lieutenant Étienne Mantour
Mort au Champ d'Honneur

It is delightful to know that when the police of Paris
temporarily abandoned their normal occupation of com-
bating the criminal population of Paris and took to fighting
the Germans instead, the former, the criminals, also
struck work. They halted their usual labours, no matter
how profitable, explaining, " *Mais, Messieurs,* we also are
Frenchmen. We are Parisians too." I think they resumed
work on August 26th after General Leclerc and General
de Gaulle had entered the city in triumph; though it is
possible that the opportunities for a resumption of labour
during the uproarious rejoicings when the crowds were
crammed shoulder to shoulder in boulevards and streets,
and mansions and shops stood empty awhile, were not
neglected. After all, the victory was won now.

You must look also at the ten small plaques side by side
on the corner of the Tuileries Garden wall, just where the
Rue de Rivoli enters the Place de la Concorde. The citizens
of Paris, need one say, " took to the barricades " directly
the National Council of the Resistance called them from
their secret lairs to open rebellion. And here these ten
squares of marble tell you how, on the last but one of the
eight great days, and in the last battle for Paris, ten fell at
this point, even as Paris was being set free. They include
a man of the F.F.I. (*Forces Françaises Intérieures*), an *étudiant
en Pharmacie*, a fireman, a first-aid man, and a red cross
nurse. " *Tombé héroiquement,*" say the stones ... " *Tombé
glorieusement âgé de 21 ans* ... *Madeline Brunet, Infirmière de la
Croix Rouge Morte pour la France.*"

Lastly, before we leave the Resistance and the Eight
Heroic Days of Paris, we must pay our visit to the church

of St. Roch in the Rue St. Honoré. This famous seven-
teenth- and eighteenth-century church has many claims to
our notice but while we speak of the Resistance we can
deal with only one. It is remarkable for bearing on its
heavy Doric and Corinthian façade marks which link the
Revolution and Napoleon to the Resistance and the
Liberation.

Go up its wide steps towards the most westerly of its
three arched entrances, remembering as you go that they
and the threshold above them were once crowded with
the spectators who watched, as from a grandstand, the
tumbril of Marie Antoinette go by, and at other times, all too
often, with the mob that hooted and spat at Charlotte
Corday, Danton, Desmoulins, Robespierre, Madame Roland
and at the Girondins singing as they passed. Remembering
all this, look at the corner between façade and stairway wall
and see it pitted everywhere with bullet marks or chippings
made by cannon. These are a script almost cuneiform
incised by the hand of the young General Bonaparte who,
on the 13th Vendémiaire an IV (October 5th, 1795) cleared
these steps of a counter-revolutionary mob with a murderous fire from muskets and artillery. This was the
" whiff of grapeshot " that ended the Revolution, " blowing
it," in Carlyle's words, " into space." But there are also,
so they say, among these writings of Napoleon other
scars made during the street fighting of 1944, and who
shall distinguish now between the wounds of 1795 and
those of 1944?

Enter the church by this westerly door and go as far as
the third chapel on your left. This is the chapel of those
who must never be forgotten when we speak of the
Resistance. It is consecrated to the memory of a hundred
thousand men and women who were deported from France
between 1942 and 1945 and died in the German concentration camps at Buchenwald, Dachau, Auschwitz, Belsen,
Ravensbrück and elsewhere, the Chapelle des Martyrs de

la Déportation. A tricolour flag droops over a large stone which says, " Here their ashes recall those deported, the victims of the Nazis, 1940–1945."

It is perhaps noteworthy that this simple commemorative wall, with its drooping tricolour, does not, like some tremendous monuments in Père Lachaise, speak of men " *torturés et fusillés par les Allemands. France, souviens toi.*" It says only, " Victims of the *Nazis* " and ends with words from a prayer of St. Francis of Assisi, " Lord, make me an instrument of your peace."

The closing paragraph of this fine story of the Paris Resistance is written on the balustrade of the Hôtel de Ville. Here a large white stone tablet stares out at the Place de l'Hôtel de Ville which has witnessed so many stormy scenes and which, as the place of executions, when it sloped roughly downward to the Seine, saw so many die on gibbet, block, stake, rack, and wheel. The stone tablet bears the heading: *Le Gouvernement Provisoire décerne la Croix de la Libération à la Ville de Paris* and in its lovely French tongue then speaks of a *capitale fidèle à elle-même.*

" A capital faithful to itself and to France has manifested beneath the enemy's occupation and oppression, and in despite of voices of surrender and treachery, her steadfast resolution to fight and to conquer. . . . By her courage in the presence of the invader, and by the indomitable energy with which she endured the most cruel ordeals she has deserved to remain the exemplar *pour la nation tout entière.*"

One word more. When the whole F.F.I. of Paris rose on that August 19th, it was under the command of a mysterious " Colonel Rol "; he controlled the whole width of the rising from the sewers and underground tunnels of the city. " Colonel Rol " was a metal-worker of thirty-six, Henri-Georges-René Tanguy, and he, " Colonel Rol," together with General Leclerc, at noon on the 25th in the Préfecture, received back his city from the Germans.

12

Through the Eyes of Baudelaire

12

Through the Eyes of Baudelaire

Lᴇᴛ that paragraph on its Town Hall balustrade close also the far longer story of a capital that, alike in its passionate angers and stormy virtues, its ever-resurgent vivacity, gaiety and wit, its love of art and intellect and fervent polemical conflict, all its strange elusive qualities which make it different from any other capital in Europe, has always, in the main, been faithful to itself.

Where is there a city so perfectly patterned, and patterned thus for more than a thousand years? This everlasting pattern is one statement of its eternal loyalty to itself. Consider the pattern again. Here, for sixteen centuries, is a central island divided into half for God and half for Caesar; a great church and its precincts at its eastern end, and a Palais de Justice, once the palace of the king, in the west. The city's river, encircling this island, sweeps right through the city's midst so that its thirty bridges unite two equal parts instead of wandering adrift like Thames and Tiber and leaving all the splendour aside on a single bank. The palaces, domes and greater churches are hardly less magnificent on the southern bank than on the northern. Architecture is just as joyously at home on the hill of St. Geneviève and the plain of Issy as anywhere on the plain beneath the shoulders of Montmartre; remember only, and it is enough, the domes of the Invalides, the Institut, the Sorbonne and Val-de-Grâce; the façades of the Palais Bourbon, the Palais du Luxembourg, and the Panthéon. The city's wide boulevards encompass it and cross it, leading nearly always to some great civic monument or historic church or palace. Even the vice and squalor, inescapable in a city of millions, are fairly divided between Right Bank and Left, dwelling happily " with splendours and miseries " in the Marais district under Montmartre and at the feet of St. Geneviève's " mountain," around the Rue de l'Hirondelle, the Rue de la Huchette, and the Rue Mazarine.

As I recall in my chair the streets of Paris I see them both sun-caught and shadowed; and this because the road-ways and trottoirs are narrow but the houses high, so that the bright sun of Paris, shining through the limpid air, washes only the upper parts with light. For most of the day the shadows of the houses on the unlit sides fall across the tall houses opposite, as on a screen. Not in the broad boulevards, of course; here the shadows lie more often on the ground, dappled and restless, beneath the plane or chestnut trees. One of the charms of the narrower streets, as you cross their mouths walking along a boulevard, is that you can catch at the far end of so many of them a glimpse of the sunlit domes and tower of Sacré Coeur, rising into the sky like Bunyan's Celestial City.

> So, I mused, (sang our Elizabeth Barrett Browning)
> Up and down, up and down, the terraced streets,
> The glittering boulevards, the white colonnades
> Of fair, fantastic Paris who wears boughs
> Like plumes, as if man made them—tossing up
> Her fountains in the sunshine from the squares,
> As dice i' the game of beauty, sure to win. . . .

We tried to see the Bois through the eyes of Proust; perhaps we may take our last sight of Paris through the eyes of Charles Baudelaire, poor fantastic little sinner and great poet. Baudelaire, in the time of the Second Empire, was as completely a poet of Paris as Proust its novelist in a later day. As he walks the streets in his black broadcloth with his hands deep in its pockets and his extremely high hat perched on an abundance of hair, his eyes are usually tranced with thought because he is endeavouring, according

to his notions of what great poetry should be, to distil everything he sees, let it be never so commonplace, so ugly, so repellent, into some vision, some shape of thought, that is a "beauty of the spirit." "*Tu m'as donne ta boue et j'en ai fait de l'or.*" "Thou hast given me thy mud and I have made it into gold." As Dr. Enid Starkie, a fine student of Baudelaire, has said, he was one of the first and greatest of the poets to be inspired by a modern capital city; and his "Parisian Pictures" in his *Fleurs du Mal* are among the most successful in that haunting book. "He was the first," she says, "to see the beauty of the teeming modern city; to see beauty also in the dim little lives of those who inhabited these vast conglomerations."

He stood to watch the dawn break over Paris when "the air is filled with the quiver of things that escape away."

> Dawn, a-shiver with cold, in mantle of rose and green,
> Came gently, slowly, along the deserted Seine,
> And this old grey Paris, rubbing its eyes from sleep,
> Stretched a hand for its tools, like a labouring man, now old.

Or he watched the dark come down over Paris.

> Oh, evening, lovable evening, desire of him
> Whose arms can say, nor lie, " Today
> We have worked." It is evening that solaces
> The spirits devoured by ravaging grief,
> The stubborn scholar whose brow is heavy now,
> And the bowed labourer who wins his bed again.

But meanwhile:

> Prostitution lights up in the streets.
> As an ant-hill she opens all her doors
> And everywhere spawns in her secret way
> Like an enemy who attempts the sudden assault;
> She stirs on the breast of this city of mud. . . .

So it may be, but his last thought in this poem is one of compassion.

> *Encore la plupart n'ont ils jamais connu*
> *La douceur du foyer et n'ont jamais vécu.*

So much for the streets; on the whole I think our last sight of Paris, a Baudelairean view, should be taken at sundown from the hump of one of the thirty bridges that make the city one. Resting your arms on the eastern parapet of—let us say the Pont du Carrousel because here we shall have Voltaire on one side of us, and the Kings on the other—you will see the Seine's sparkling floor stippled as in a pointillist picture with all the colours of sunset, rose and green and mauve, and beyond the other noble bridges the Gothic towers of Notre Dame, the cone-capped towers of the

14—P

Conciergerie, and the slender flèche of St. Louis' Sainte Chapelle, all on the Isle of the Cité, which rides on its river like a ship with its prow towards us. And this, remember, was the Parisii's little wet island of willows, rushes, and round thatched huts.

You will see the long river quays shadowed by their chestnut trees and almost certainly (for when are they not there?) the anglers immobile and contemplative behind their long rods of hope and their lines which are so still. For sure you will see the lovers shamelessly embracing on a withdrawn seat or against the trunk of a tree; they fear no *voyeur's* watching from the fishing men, for these have a love of their own. I think you will also see one or two of the " clochards " of Paris, those bedraggled and picturesque hobos who know where upon the quays or under the bridges there are fair places to sleep. Your ears catch the whistle of distant tugs, heading perhaps for Rouen; the pant of an unseen motor-boat; and the sudden flutter of a pigeon's wings; while from below the bridge before you, the Pont de Solferino, comes a long pleasure boat, one of the Bateaux Mouches, crowded with sightseers from every country speaking twenty tongues. Wearing for the first time today, now that twilight is at hand, its girdle of illuminations, it brings with it, and leaves behind it, the wet-reed smell of the Seine. Nor is it impossible that, at sudden moments, you may hear and see wild ducks fall upon the river, feet-first, like flagged forms, russet-green, blown out of the sky.

And all this time you stand enclosed, as it were, in a frame of ever undulating sound, a low humming and a whispering; it is the ceaseless rumour and sighing of the cars on the long cream-stone quays and on the bridges before and behind you. It could be the very sound of Time itself, heeded only seldom but ebbing away for ever into the secrecy of the past.

There is always a strange healing, somehow, in such a river scene with one of man's most monumental cities for its background—did not Wordsworth feel the same, looking on London from a bridge?—and I have a fancy that Baudelaire wrote his most beautiful poem, *Recueillement,* in such a place and at such an hour.

> Be still, my Sorrow; oh my Grief, be wise,
> You cried for evening; it falls, and it is here.
> A dimming air the town encompasses
> Bearing its peace to some; to others care.
>
> And while the poor, base, mortal horde,
> Whipped on by Pleasure, their unsparing lord,
> Find only sadness in their foolish play,
> Give me thy hand, oh Sorrow. Come this way,
>
> Come far, to where the worn old agonies
> Lean forward from the sky's high terraces,
> And where Regret mounts, smiling, from the deeps.
>
> The dying sun beneath an archway sleeps,
> And like a winding sheet for those that die
> Oh, hear, dear Grief, the soft sweet night is nigh.

Index